THE TRANSCENDENTAL EXPLOSION

by
John Weldon
and
Zola Levitt

HARVEST HOUSE PUBLISHERS
Irvine, California

THE TRANSCENDENTAL EXPLOSION

FOREWORD

In the entertainment world, TM has been popular for some time. One of my own musicians did his best to involve me and my daughters in Transcendental Meditation, and made the tactical mistake of giving me a couple of cassette tapes by a "meditation master." My musician friend thought I'd be impressed with the intellectual prowess of this Ph.D. who had progressed so far toward his personal nirvana, or "cosmic consciousness." It didn't occur to him that perhaps the Bible already had some specific things to say about the principles of Transcendental Meditation—or that I might be aware of what the Bible has to say on the subject.

All I had to hear to turn me away forever was the "meditation master," in answer to an interested disciple's question, stating positively that anyone throughout intensive and prolonged meditation, could progress to the level of God—or God-consciousness and God-oneness—in one lifetime! Normally, he said, it would take several lifetimes for a dedicated guru or meditating spirit to become one with God, *knowing all things* (wasn't Eve promised something like that by the cunning beast of Eden?). So automatically, reincarnation and arriving at God's level through one's own efforts were part and parcel of TM. I tried to show my friend what the Bible had to say on this subject, but to my dismay, the Bible was no longer the final authority on anything, and he was "hooked" on TM. We parted company shortly after that.

This book will underscore and expose all you need to know about Transcendental Meditation, its dangers and fallacies. I don't know if you will accept all of the author's conclusions, but surely you will be forced to see this national rage as much more than a harmless way to relax. I, personally, am indebted to John and Zola for their deep analytical research. I believe they have done a great service for all of us, and they write in a crisp and breezy way that gives life to their painstaking analysis.

If you're really interested in inner tranquility and cosmic joy—here's the recipe:

"And let the peace of Christ rule in your hearts, to which indeed you were called in one body; and be thankful.

"Let the Word of Christ richly dwell within you; with all wisdom teaching and admonishing one another with psalms and hymns and spiritual songs, singing with thankfulness in your hearts to God.

"And whatever you do in word or deed, do all in the name of the Lord Jesus, giving thanks to Him through God the Father." (Col. 3:15-17)

Pat Boone

"To those who recognize that within themselves cannot be found all that may be required of them for time and eternity."

ABOUT THE AUTHORS

John Weldon received his B.A. degree with honors from California State University of San Diego in 1972, graduating with distinction in Sociology. He has been a research editor and is presently on the faculty of The Light and Power House, a Biblical Training School near the UCLA campus in Westwood, California. He spent hundreds of hours researching this book on TM and at one time was actively involved in meditation going through the actual TM *puja*—or initiation rite. He co-authored with Zola Levitt *UFO's: What On Earth Is Happening?*

Zola Levitt, a Hebrew Christian, graduated from Duquesne and Indiana Universities in Music. He has a Ph.D. from Indiana, and has performed with the New Orleans Philharmonic, San Antonio Symphony Orchestras and Glen Campbell Show tours. He is a marriage counselor and member-in-training for Psychoanalysis. At one time, Levitt studied with a Yoga master and performed physical exercises, meditation, and the study of *Koans*—the mind-murdering riddles of Zen. He met the Lord in 1971, and is now a Christian author with over a dozen books in print, lecturer and radio talk show host.

Due to his schedule, Mr. Weldon regrets he can answer only a small portion of mail received.

CONTENTS

1. The Transcendental Explosion 12
2. Dark Days in the Lab 33
3. That Old-Time Religion 52
4. The TM Mystique 79
5. A Bad Trip 99
6. The Manson Factor 128
7. Some Dissatisfied Customers 154
8. Maharishi or Jesus: Which Way to God? 173

Appendix 1. TM Mantras and Hindu Gods 190
Appendix 2. TM and the Occult 195
Appendix 3. TM, Yoga, and the Serpent Power 206
Appendix 4. TM, Reincarnation, and the Bible 214

ACKNOWLEDGMENTS

I would like especially to thank Brooks Alexander and Dave Fetcho of the Spiritual Counterfeits Project, P.O. Box 4308, Berkeley, California 94704, a research group dedicated to the exposure of the deceptive religious cults of our day. Their sacrificial work should be supported in every way possible. Gifts are tax-deductible. I would also like to thank Chuck Ashman, Vail Hamilton, Yvonne Maher, Mike Minder, Leon Otis, Greg Randolph, Mick Van Buskirk, John Vos and Joan Wheeler for their help in various ways. Finally, I would like to express my genuine appreciation to Claudia Bausman, for her godliness and encouragement.

John Weldon

THE TRANSCENDENTAL EXPLOSION

"I do not see anything. I do not know anything. Nothing remains. What remains is Bliss."

Maharishi

"Spiritual seeking has clearly reached the proportions of a national trend. Everyone seems to be looking for the answer. So were the people of Germany during the 20's when there was widespread fascination with the occult and a higher rate of Indian gurus per capita than even in the U.S. today.

I ask myself, "Are we, at the New Age Journal, in the vanguard of a great social awakening, or are we blindly leading a rush to judgment? Are these times truly unprecedented, or is the New Age simply this season's version of life's same old soap opera? How can we gain a sense of history and a measure of common sense? Where have we come from, who are we, where are we going?"

Eric Utne, Editor, *New Age Journal*

"It seems increasingly likely that our whole culture may swing Eastwards in its underlying presuppositions about life."

Dr. R. D. Clements

"There is a great need to be realistic and critical about what we are. We must not be spiritually gullible."

Chogyam Trungpa

"The real nature of life is absolute bliss-consciousness.... Man is born of bliss.... Life is bliss."

Maharishi Mahesh Yogi

"A former president of the Norwegian Academy of Sciences, helped by historians from Britain, Egypt, Germany, and India, and using an electronic computer, has found that since 3600 B.C. the world has known only 292 years of peace. In this period of more than 55 centuries, there have been 14,531 wars, large and small, in which more than 3.6 billion people were killed. Since 650 B.C. there have been 1, 656 arms races, all except 16 ending in war, and these 16 ended in economic collapse for the countries concerned."

(Stockton Record)

CHAPTER ONE

THE TRANSCENDENTAL EXPLOSION

Look out! Here comes another ''New Age of Enlightenment.''

We're due for ''a permanent state of harmony, happiness and peace in the world,'' according to Guru Maharishi Mahesh Yogi, as soon as he gets enough people to practice his transcendental meditation.[1] Our troubles will be over, according to the guru.

Students of past ''new ages'' will have little trouble recognizing the signs. Any number of past changers of the world order have made the same promises.

Maharishi's ''New Age'', as a recent private publication of his movement informs us, will be characterized by an extended state of peace on earth. ''The history of world wars has already ended,'' but this is only the beginning. The time is ''not far off'' when even minor skirmishes will be a thing of the past, and when 5% of the world's people are meditating, a la Maharishi, ''The family of nations will be completely without fears.'' Not only will war be eliminated, but mankind's more pervasive enemy, disease, will also be banished forever. The perfect health of society and every individual member will be a natural feature of the New Age of Enlightenment.[2]

The publication, circulated only to in-group TM devotees, concludes that all the world's troubles are presently brought about by faulty, non-evolutionary thinking. When human beings gain a new comprehension of nature and evolution, by TM methods, men will more closely adhere to the true laws of nature, as explained by the guru, and everybody will be satisfied.[3]

Well, not quite everybody. There is a group, called by the guru, "the unfit," who may not be at all happy when the New Age comes in.

DOWN WITH THE UNFIT!

The perennial hindrance to great new ages—the folks who don't want to participate—will have to be disposed of somehow. Maharishi thinks nature will take care of them and provide "non-existence for the unfit". In his words:

There has not been and there will not a place for the unfit. The fit will lead, and if the unfit are not coming along, there is no place for them. In the place where light dominates there is no place for darkness. In the Age of Enlightenment there is no place for ignorant people. The ignorant will be made enlightened by a few orderly, enlightened people moving around. Nature will not allow ignorance to prevail. It just can't. Non-existence of the unfit has been the law of nature.[4]

This ruthless side of the bright New Age to come is nothing new for bright new ages. Peaceful TM, hailed as the quiet way to inner peace and fulfillment, has a very dark side, it would appear. So do most other grandiose plans for world peace. There always seems to be some sort of elite group who will lead everyone else around by their noses, or even cut off their noses altogether. Those identified as "unfit" by the guru, rather like those considered unfit by military dictators, are inevitably in for a bad time of it when the new order comes in.

Those "few orderly, enlightened people moving a-round," helping us ignorant ones in the New Age, some-how evoke images of regimentation typical of the enforce-ment of peace that so invariably accompanies social "im-provement." A few orderly, enlightened Communists have enslaved half the world at this point, and world peace is nowhere in sight. The orderly folk of the Third Reich couldn't seem to stop killing people in their enthusiasm to help them out.

The true attitude of the guru and his real plans for the future are not available to the general public. The TM promoters do not explain very widely the whole truth about their plans. This book is designed to tell the inside story, from TM's own publications, meetings, the testimonies of meditators and the voluminous writings of Master Mahar-ishi himself.

WHAT IS TM?

Transcendental meditation is a somewhat simplified yoga technique designed to alter one's consciousness. After three introductory lectures and payment of the standard fee of $125, one is eligible for initiation into TM. During a subsequent fifteen minute Hindu *puja*, or initiation cere-mony, the beginner receives his supposedly individual, secret mantra, the mysterious sound he will meditate on. Co-author John Weldon followed this procedure some years ago, receiving the mantra "ieng."

From then on the new devotee is to meditate twice daily for fifteen or twenty minutes each time, meditating solely on the mantra. This process is supposed to take the mind through increasingly subtle levels of thought down to the very subtlest level of conscious thought. Then there is a transcendance, going beyond, to "the field of pure creative intelligence," or "absolute bliss consciousness," in the argot of the movement.

Several times during the meditation period the devotee will realize that his mantra is no longer there and that he is aware of nothing but "awareness" itself. This is referred to as "pure awareness," the ultimate goal of TM. TM is designed to take one to the "source of all thought," "pure creative intelligence," etc.

When the devotee is experiencing the source of all thought, he is to ease back to the mantra, meditating on it again and returning slowly to where he started. Whatever may happen in the mind during this "traveling" is to be left alone; it is all a part of TM and all to the good. The devotee is merely to follow the procedure; the process will take care of itself.

This "diving into the depths of the mind" is what Maharishi calls reaching "Being". Traveling through the depths infuses the mind of the meditator with more and more Being, until the very nature of the mind becomes transformed *into* Being. Conceivably the initiate may learn to "stay down" where his meditation has taken him—maintaining the state of Being. This is apparently to be desired.

We will discuss this strange state of Being further in Chapter Four along with the negative side which its promotors do their best to hide from the public.

THE IMPACT OF TM

With its stunning impact on American society and its far

15

ranging effect on the rest of the world, the popularity of TM can hardly be overestimated.

Current initiations in this country alone are running at thirty to fifty thousand *per month* at this writing![5] Close to one million people have become practicers of TM in the United States, with 10,000 teachers operative and hundreds of research projects underway on the subject. The federal government of our country has funded at least seventeen such TM research projects.[6]

TM has set up an international controlling organization known as the World Plan Executive Council (WPEC), and presently five American Organizations operate under its auspices. The Spiritual Regeneration Movement (SRM), Students International Meditation Society (SIMS), the International Meditation Society (IMS), the Foundation for the Science of Creative Intelligence (FSCI) and Maharishi International University (MIU) are all American installations of the international TM movement.

The structure of the movement is very well organized, with each member group serving its peculiar function. Among the American organizations, for example, FSCI is concerned with research and IMS with reaching the business community. The attempt is being made for TM to reach every nook and cranny of American society. There is even an SCI course for elementary schools, where children as young as four years of age can begin to meditate in the TM way.

The permeation of U.S. society by TM is extremely successful, with public non-TM organizations, in addition to the federal government, helping its progress. The National Institute of Mental Health recently awarded a grant of $21,500 to finance the TM training of 150 high school teachers. A $72,000 grant by the National Institute of Alcohol Abuse and Alcoholism is currently funding a TM project in the District of Columbia. The United States Army has promoted TM as beneficial for its personnel, and there is a meditation room for junior officers in the Pentagon.[7] High-ranking officers, even some generals and admirals, publicize the fact that they meditate, and thereby recommend TM to the multitudes.

There have been more than 150 local government proclamations endorsing TM, including proposals and endorsements in state governments and even in the United States Senate.[8] WPEC will doubtless make good use of the U.S. government stamp of approval in its worldwide activities if Senate Resolution 64, intended to increase public awareness of TM passes. Maharishi has come by invitation to address several state legislatures and has received standing ovations.

TM centers have been established on more than one thousand college campuses throughout the United States, and SCI, which teaches the theoretical side of the procedure, is widely offered for credit on both high school and college campuses. TM courses have been given at American-owned corporations with international outreach (there are TM centers in ninety countries in addition to the four hundred such centers in the United States) AT&T, General Foods and a number of other powerful American corporations have undertaken such training programs.[9] Chris Hegarty, an executive sales trainer for some of the most prestigious American firms, says, ''I could give you a list of hundreds of corporation presidents and other important persons who believe that it really works and has changed their lives.''[10]

Entertainers endorse TM widely on talkshows and even during performances. The Beach Boys, a musical group, give veritable lectures after their concerts and urge initiation into TM for everybody. Beach Boy Mike Love, is reportedly giving TM lessons to Senators Ted Kennedy and John Tunney in their Senate offices; they are two of a long list of political leaders who practice TM.''[11]

With government officials in the United States personally utilizing TM, and other countries assisting WPEC to set up their local installations (Brazilian officials are working with the international TM headquarters group to establish nine-ty-eight Plan centers in their nation; Nepal has officially endorsed TM for every level of its society),[12] TM is moving into the international community at an impressive pace. Even the United Nations may promote TM through a resolution of endorsement currently being considered. Only casually examined by many of its neophyte adherents, it is sweeping the world like a new religion.

But it's not a new religion. It's actually a very old religion, as we will see.

A TM TAKEOVER?

TM is moving faster and in more influential circles than almost any spiritual idea in history. Maharishi, a talented and shrewd promoter, is apparently going for all the marbles. The American presidency would satisfy him—that is to say, he would like to see a TM-supporting man in office. His ambitions are even greater than that, however. His Age of Enlightenment vision takes in the entire world, of course, but a meditating United States president might be a helpful step to bigger things.

It's not so far-fetched. According to TM sources, there are presently a few very strong contenders for the presidency who meditate. Birch Bayh, a potential presidential hopeful, is also interested in TM.[13]

Maharishi is rather more up-to-date than the usual sitting guru, utilizing particularly the television medium to prom-ulgate his doctrine. Channel 18 KSCI-TV in Los Angeles, a TM station, broadcasts taped lectures by the master himself to a potential audience of six million. There are plans for six more TV stations in the next four years by the TM advocates, whose excitement over their product knows no bounds.

The guru wants to form a global color TV network! He

recently sent every head of state *in the world* his "Alliance for Knowledge," a plan to bring TM into every household on the planet.

TV personalities and well-known personages in general, including Joe Namath, Stevie Wonder, Efrem Zimbalist Jr., Merv Griffin, Clint Eastwood, Peggy Lee, Bill Walton and Samantha Jones, are paraded as endorsing TM. Claire Pittman, Information Officer for the Department of Health, Education and Welfare, meditates; Major General Franklin Davis meditates. Almost everybody who is anybody who meditates is going to be touted by Maharishi in his powerful media outreach. After all, if the stars do it....

Psychotherapists in some quarters regard TM as very beneficial, and a few of these impressionable healers have suggested that TM might be a useful adjunct to much of the current effort of the psychotherapeutic community.[14] Psychiatrist Harold Bloomfield, sounding not unlike his guru, says, "The great transformation of our society is silently in progress. The TM program is spreading extremely quickly but also very quietly."[15] The psychiatrist compares the TM impact to that of the Industrial Revolution, and lauds Maharishi's plan "to make the TM program available to everyone on earth."[16]

Maharishi is not trying to be nearly as quiet as the doctor thinks. He is, in fact, trying to make a very big noise in the world. But not everyone is a meditator after his sort. Westerners have much to meditate on, and dissenters, unfit as they may seem to the purists, simply do not always go for transcendental solutions to real problems. Maharishi's ways are disagreeably "Eastern" to many Americans, involving as they do an inert, inactive, alternative to active problem-solving. Still, TM is widely practiced, as we have seen, and the business community, for one down-to-earth sector, just eats it up. Dr. Francis Barrett, President of Management Concepts Ltd., Canada, predicts that within ten years the guru's Science of Creative Intelligence (SCI), styled as the intellectual study of TM, will be taught in "over fifty per cent of North American executive training programs."[17] The influence of that much TM study in that much of the commercial sector of any society would certainly be generally felt at every level.

Maharishi has not stopped with television, publishing operations, research projects, the outreach to world leaders and the legwork of setting up local centers; he has set up his own university for the ongoing teaching of his Science of Creative Intelligence. Maharishi International University, purchased from ailing Parsons College for 2.5 million dollars (after the guru "meditated" the price down from fourteen million), is a public relations factory where the students must work to spread the doctrine in order to graduate![18] The faculty varies in number, no D's or F's are ever given, presumably in keeping with the surface gentleness of the TM style, and the subject matter is seen through Maharishi's philosophy. Academic subjects are offered, but only in the "light" of SCI. The school is not accredited as yet but has been granted "recognized candidacy for accreditation." This is surprising, since the single-minded guru teaches that all education is meaningless and of little or no value unless interpreted through SCI.[19] The university will ultimately simply exist to promulgate the TM doctrine but will be recognized, if accredited, as equal in stature to any American university.

To envision a takeover at this point might be overdoing it, but looking at the master's progress and his ambitious techniques, it would not come as a total surprise.

Meditate on that!

HOW DOES A GURU GROW?

Maharishi Mahesh Yogi is a thorough-going Hindu, deeply studied in the philosophy of that religion and loyal to

20

its gods. The guru freely admits to that and, indeed, holds this background of TM to be its great motivating power.

According to Maharishi, TM goes all the way back to Krishna, who lived some five thousand years ago and first taught TM in the sacred Hindu book, the Bhagavad Gita. TM was lost along the way, until Buddha restored the teaching. It was somehow lost yet again, until picked up by a later sage, and so it went, coming and going throughout Hindu history. (Many would argue whether Krishna ever taught TM, to say nothing, of course, of Buddha himself.)

Maharishi says he belongs to the "blessed tradition" of Shankara,[20] one of the ancient rediscoverers of TM; and in private ceremonies he personally worships Shankara's preferred diety, Shiva.[21] Shankara pursued knowledge of Brahman, the final and highest impersonal Hindu diety,[22] and he sought to prove the reality of Brahman and the unreality of everything else, rather a characteristic of Maharishi himself. The modern TM guru seems to see perfect invalidity all around him and trusts only in TM.

The ancient *rishis,* occultists or seers, received "revelations" supernaturally and were not too concerned with finding the truth of things through reason; they depended on "deeper consciousness." Their revelations became the Vedas, sacred Hindu writ. Maharishi ties himself to this tradition—actually Vedanta, Hinduism in the tradition of Shankara—and terms it "The Holy Tradition.[23]" "For all this knowledge," says the guru in gratitude, "my indebtedness is to the holy tradition of Jagadguru Bhagwan Shankaracharya (Shankara), the main source of all my inspirations and activity.[24]"

Surely the guru, sharp trader that he is, owes something to the techniques of modern public relations as well, but to take him at his word, he is merely the modern instrument of an ancient, respected Hindu tradition. The fruits of ancient Hinduism, profound as they once may have been, are not very impressive today. One sees hardly any sort of practical enlightenment among the present day Hindus, and a new age of peace must be far off.

But perhaps the new guru's modern improvements will step up the progress toward the new age. His own study was with a more up-to-date guru in India. The twentieth-century swami, Brahmananda Sarasivati, known as Guru Dev (Divine Teacher), was Maharishi's Master. A veteran of Hindu self-discipline, Dev spent some sixty years in Himalayan caves and jungles meditating!

When Dev at length finished his meditations and returned to take the venerated northern seat of Shankara, Maharishi approached him and became his disciple. He did everything to be close to his guru, to ''breathe his air.'' Maharishi soon became the Master's favorite follower, and upon his death in 1953, Guru Dev commissioned his faithful disciple to devise a simple technique for God-realization for the masses.

This was quite an interesting problem, and Maharishi withdrew to a cave to think about it. Unlike his Master, he came back quickly with the whole answer, and in two years Maharishi was teaching TM in southern India. Not nearly the marathon meditator his own guru was, Maharishi nevertheless felt very confident of his system and psychically very encouraged.

The southern India experiment was a false start; somehow the new guru's simple techniques did not appeal to his countrymen. But his world wide movement, begun in 1957, has been a roaring success, ''quietly.'' Conceivably, the Maharishi version of efficient cave sitting and simplified meditating appealed more widely to jittery western minds. Guru Dev would have had some trouble marketing his profundities in the west, with all due respect to his enormous personal sacrifices.

The disciples Maharishi has been able to collect, in their number and importance, would have been the envy of many of his gods. Their loyalty is unquestionable and their respect for their master unflinching and unqualified. As psychiatrist

Dr. Byron Rigby says:

> Perfect order in one member of a vast population is sufficient to enlighten the whole population. This one person is Maharishi Mahesh Yogi. The whole world, the whole cosmos, owes an enormous debt of gratitude to the great line of (Hindu) Masters and to Guru Dev who have been able to give us the wonderful gift of Maharishi.[25]

The religious overtones of this testimonial and many others like it in the promotional literature of TM, are the major concern of this book. The authors feel that Maharishi is actually offering Hinduism carefully gift-wrapped as some sort of modern psychological breakthrough. Since loyalty to the eastern dieties is heavily involved in the practice of TM, as the above testimonial clearly states, Maharishi may well be one of the ''end times'' false prophets foretold by Jesus (Matt. 24:24 etc.). According to biblical prophecy, we are to expect a heightening of interest in worldly religious systems as the ''end times'' approach. Certainly the presence of ''perfect messiahs,'' dispensers of ''divine light,'' gurus of every stripe and an increasing interest in occult practices has been manifest in the past few years. Maharishi, with all of his utopian promises and ambitious plans, fits the biblical picture of things to come.

A TM UTOPIA?

The scope of what the TM guru expects from his system is overwhelming.[26] His brand of meditation is meant to introduce solutions to the world's most intricate and persistent problems. TM offers utopia—a virtual heaven on earth.

World peace is only the first of a long line of knotty problems which TM will solve, according to its adherents. TM will produce perfectly integrated human beings—socially, psychologically and physically perfect people. TM will do away with all suffering in life. Maharishi claims that TM is "an effective cure for mental illness" and will even lead to increased agricultural production and better food crops through TM-effected control of the weather![27]

That's only the beginning. TM will produce a new kind of human being who will have greater intelligence and energy, be filled with inner peace and "all knowledge" (including eternal freedom, bliss, creativity and fulfillment, to quote the guru's writings) and be *infallible*. Maharishi claims that TM stops physical decay during meditation and that it will thus transform men "into The Divine.[28]"

Men are to be like God:

The Science of Creative Intelligence structures all knowledge in the awareness of everyone and thereby makes everyone infallible. [29]

The happiest news is that a meditating population of merely one percent in any given society will be sufficient to produce significant changes in that society. At five percent, things will *really* begin to happen. The meditators will have the jump on everybody else because of their infallibility, power, more orderly minds, etc. Every action the meditators perform will have a beneficent effect in every corner of the universe. [30]

THAT SAME OLD SONG AND DANCE

To an increasing number of people, however, TM promises nothing beneficial at all and amounts to the same sort of "better world ahead" promises that mankind has been hearing since the day some ancient ancestor carved his first idol. The revering of the Hindu faith is not likely to produce anything more than the Hindus have gotten out of it, and a close inspection of the TM movement shows the same human failings and bickerings that plague all such easy-millennium systems. It seems like that same old song and dance again.

TM training camps are experiencing the very unexpected phenomena of friction between the seasoned meditators, inability to coordinate the goals of the movement, and even committed meditators being fired from their jobs. If a five percent mix of TM devotees is supposed to change the whole society some day, it is remarkable that a hundred percent saturation runs into such bad luck. Perhaps the mixture is too rich.

And on that point, the Maharishi, like all rich men, has run into the very down-to-earth western problems of taxes and the legality of his system. The TM corporation is registered as a public charity and claims to be a "non-profit, tax exempt institution for education." It does have its commercial side, however, as it collected in the United States alone some $60 million from 1970 to 1975.[31] In the 1973-74 report of the California Attorney General's Office, it was revealed that the guru invests his money and makes it grow very much like any profit-making businessman. WPEC reportedly had a surprising stock portfolio, holding 300 shares of Commonwealth Edison, 1,000 shares of Walt Disney Productions, and additional shares of Minnesota Power and Light, Affiliated Food Distributors and Pacific Gas and Electric.[32] In view of Maharishi's commercial side, TM has lost its free-use privileges in the Los Angeles Public Libraries and some schools.[33]

Either the guru has found a way to make his remarkable system perform against the market effectively, or he has found some typically western-style philosophy to his liking.

TM is running into legal problems of many sorts as it goes onward with its quiet take over. The American legal system is built to watch for such excesses, and the guru and his followers have had a few troubles with it.

The TM promoters lost a case involving the San Lorenzo School District in northern California by running up against the separation of church and state principle. TM was threatened with a suit that was supported by the Spiritual Conterfeits Project in Berkeley.[34] It argued that

TM is Hinduism, pure and simple, and thus could neither be supported by public funds nor taught in public schools. The school district chose not to argue the case and agreed never to teach TM in the schools again.

A similar suit has been filed in Federal court in New Jersey, naming as defendants the United States government (which supplied $40,000 in funds to teach TM in the public schools) as well as the TM organization and Maharishi.

Consumer fraud laws are the question in the state of Iowa, where the attorney general has begun investigation of the TM movement. Lately, several state resolutions attempting to officially endorse or support TM have died in committee as a result of heavy public pressure against the movement. The California Concurrent Assembly Resolution 66 and New Jersey's Assembly Resolution 47 were both defeated by a public a bit wary of the guru's machinations. The *Alliance Witness* of January 14, 1976, ran this statement:

> TM's religious basis exposed in Fairfield: When the Maharishi International University (teaching Transcendental Meditation) opened last year in Fairfield, Iowa (see 4/9 issue), relations were good between the townspeople and the school. However, when the Fairfield *Ledger* printed the English translation of the *puja*, the Vedic hymn of worship sung in Sanskrit by TM instructors during the initiation rites for new students, seven Fairfield ministers asked the Iowa Attorney General to prosecute the University on charges of consumer fraud for marketing TM as a ''scientific practice.'' The translation revealed the previously secret *puja* to be worship of Guru Dev, the Maharishi Mahesh Yogi's dead Master. The items brought by initiates are offered to Guru Dev, thus involving the initiate in worship. Meanwhile, because of concern over the introduction of TM as a pilot course in some New Jersey schools, the New Jersey State Department of Education is asking the State Attorney

General to determine whether or not the system is a religion.

Also, in a recent nationwide news release issued by the Coalition for Religious Integrity, Albert J. Menendez, Director of Research for Americans United for Separation of Church and State, stated:

> TM is merely a subtly disguised form of Hinduism. The continuation of such programs in our schools clearly violates the constitution.
>
> Americans United has been in the forefront of the fight for a governmental structure free of sectarian influence. Our actions have resulted in significant court decisions voiding the expenditure of tax dollars on religious programs.
>
> *We consider the presence of TM in our American school system as among the most blatant and insidious examples of constitutional violation we have ever seen.* [35] [italics mine)

Suit has been filed in the Federal court with the possibility of a Supreme Court decision.

The troubles within the movement are coming to light as TM factions clash. Transcendental Meditation Club president Van Lenetine of Massachusetts' Framingham College recently resigned his post, froze all funds and stopped all organization publicity because, as he stated, the TM movement "engages in esoteric deception, fraud and religious connections.[36]"

Some knowledgeable people are growing suspicious of TM and its pervasive grip on this country. "Transcendental Meditation seems to be taking a firm hold on the American mind," observed the *New York Times*,[37] but some Americans have been less than eager to embrace it. T. George Harris, editor-in-chief of *Psychology Today* cautions, "If

Uncle Sam is going to bend his old knees into the lotus position, he'd better know what he'll be like when he stands up.[38]"

It has been a time-honored western tradition to test things thoroughly and to know what they are about. Americans have imported a lot of good ideas over the past two centuries, but they have also rejected many imports as false. Thalidomide comes to mind as well as foreign educational methods and commercial products that failed to meet our testing standards.

Americans have been scientifically testing TM since its inception in this country, and they have come up with some interesting data. In one sense TM is not what it's cracked up to be, and in another sense, it's much more, unfortunately.

Read on.

FOOTNOTES: CHAPTER ONE

Full documentation for a source is given the first time it is used, then only author, title and page thereafter (excludes introductory quotes).

Introductory Quotes: Issue 8, page 2; *God and the Gurus* (InterVarsity, 1975), p. 16; "An Approach to Meditation," *Journal of Transpersonal Psychology,* #1, 1973, p. 63; Maharishi, *Meditations,* p. 154-6; *On the Bhagavad Gita,* p. 311; S.F. Logsdon, *Profiles of Prophecy* (Zondervan, 1970), p. 54; Maharishi, *Love and God,* p. 30.

1. *Inauguration of the Dawn of the Age of Enlightenment,* MIU Press publication, no. G 186 c. MIU Press, 1975, pp. 7, 77, 78.

2. *Ibid.*

3. *Ibid.,* p. 59.

4. *Ibid.,* p. 47. (Unfortunately, this book provides "scientific" basis for religious racism.)

5. Western United States Regional Newsletter, Oct. 75-Jan. 76, World Plan Executive Council, Los Angeles, CA; Fairfield (Ohio) Daily Ledger, Oct. 3, 1975.

6. *Time*, Oct. 13, 1975.

7. "Spiritual Counterfeits Today," P.O. Box 4308, Berkeley, CA 94704.

8. *Inauguration . . . op. cit.* p. 80.

9. *Time*, Oct. 13, 1975.

10. David Hammond, *The Search for Psychic Power*, (Bantam, 1975) p. 213.

11. *Berkeley Barb*, Jan. 1, 1976, no. 541.

12. Exerpt from U.S. Senate Resolution 64, Congressional Record, Senate, Feb. 5, 1975, p. S1467.

13. Barb, op. cit.; Psychology Today, *April 1974, part 1.*

14. Jack Forem, *Transcendental Meditation: Maharishi Mahesh Yogi and the Science of Creative Intelligence* (Bantam, 1976), p. 136.

15. Harold Bloomfield, *TM, Discovering Inner Energy and Overcoming Stress* (Dell, 1975), p. 215.

16. *Ibid.*, p. 216.

17. *Ibid.*, p. 240.

18. Des Moines (Iowa) Sunday Register, Nov. 3, 1974, "Maharishi U: A Mecca, But Not a Harvard."

19. Maharishi, *The Seven States of Consciousness*, Liberty Records, WPS-21455 (1967); and Maharishi, *Transcendental Meditation* (Signet, 1968), pp. 209, 217.

20. *Meditations of Maharishi Mahesh Yogi* (Bantam, 1973), p. 106.

21. *Look*, Feb. 6, 1968; Ernest Wood, *Seven Schools of Yoga* (Theosophical, 1973), p. 54; Troy Organ, *Hinduism: Its Historical Development* (Barron, 1974), p. 243.

22. Swami Nikhilananda, *The Upanishads* (Harper & Row, 1964), abridged, pp. 22, 379, 384, 377.

23. Maharishi, *On the Bhagavad Gita* (Penguin, 1974), pp. 9, 11, 256; Yogi, *Meditations*, pp. 23, 45, 54-5, 133-4; "The Holy Tradition" (TM teacher puja commentary), pp. 13-14: Nikhilananda, p. 28.

24. Maharishi, *Transcendental Meditation*, p. xvii.

25. Maharishi, *Inauguration . . .*, p. 59.

26. Maharishi, *Transcendental Meditation*, pp. 112, 163, 191, 198, 297, 239-40; *Meditations*, pp. 45, 63, 87, 92, 178; *On the Bhagavad Gita*, p. 204; Denniston and McWilliams, *The TM Book* (Warner, 1975), Chs. 3, 5.

27. Maharishi, *Inauguration . . .*, pp. 55-6; Maharishi, *Transcendental Meditation*, p. 191; Maharishi, *Bhagavad Gita*, p. 204.

28. Maharishi, *Meditations*, pp. 45, 63, 87, 92; Maharishi, *Transcendental Meditation*, pp. 116, 198.

29. Maharishi, *Inauguration . . .*, p. 49.

30. Maharishi, *Transcendental Medication*, pp. 69-74; *Time*, Oct. 13, 1975; Maharishi, *Inauguration . . .*, pp. 59, 27, 77-8.

31. John White, *Everything You Want to Know About TM* (Pocket Books, 1976), p. 171.

32. "The Ashman File," Nov. 6, 1975, KTTV, Channel 11, Los Angeles, 11-11:30 p.m.

33. *Ibid.*, and their subsequent TM program (1976). (Due to solicitation of the $125.00 fee.)

34. P.O. Box 4308, Berkeley, CA 94704, "TM Legal Case Update," Dec. 20, 1975.

35. Nationwide press release of Feb. 18, 1976, from the Coalition for Religious Integrity, cf. *Time*, March 1, 1976.

36. Framingham College student paper, late 1975.

37. Anatole Broyard, March, 1975, from *The TM Book*.

38. December, 1975, p. 4.

"Life is. This exactness that is and another exactness of this isness is that it is in various phases."

—Maharishi

"Since some of the TM research is being questioned and contradicted, there may be a discrepancy of unknown proportions between what is claimed and what is actually delivered."

—John White

"It is only childish and ridiculous to base one's life on the level of thinking. Thinking can never be a profound basis of living. Being is the natural basis . . . Thinking, on the other hand, is only imaginary."

—Maharishi

"Nor should we underestimate their power; like a fungus cracking a slab of concrete by the slow relentless pressure of its growth, the anti-rationalism of our time may yet bring down science in ruin. Polyani has warned that science as we know it may be dead in fifty years."

—Anthony Campbell

"From the point of view of the Divine, problems do not exist."

—Maharishi

"Everything that comes out of the cow is sacred, including dung and urine. A dose of the mixture consisting of milk, curds, ghee (clarified butter), cow dung and urine is considered extremely purifying to the soul and to the body, and the Hindus who act up to it are many . . . . In the streets of Hindu cities, pious men and women of the lower classes may be seen following cows, catching the urine of the cow in the cupped palm of their hand and sipping it. No pious Hindu will pass a cow without . . . an act of homage."
—P. Thomas, *Hindu Religious Customs, and Manners*

CHAPTER TWO

DARK DAYS IN THE LAB

Maharishi is attempting to utilize scientific testing to back up his claim that TM provides peace, alleviation of suffering, bliss, etc., etc.. Much effort and money goes into research at TM centers in view of solidly establishing the scientific validity of the system and thus shoring it up to laboratory verified respectability in the American mind.

Though working with eastern ideals, the guru is trying to infuse western principles of unbiased examination into his program. This isn't easy. Scientific corroboration of religion or philosophy has been awfully hard to come by historically. In general, the guru and his ideas don't fit very well into the American picture of things curative.

Some American scientists write off the guru at a glance, refusing to be bothered with his cure-all formula. The head of San Francisco State University's philosophy department, Dr. Jacob Needleman, stated:

Had this dimunitive, giggling Hindu left his monastery in the Himalayas only to "bring to the west" the rosy cosmic optimism which had gasped its last in Auschwitz, Hiroshima and Viet Nam? . . . In all of this, many westerners began remembering what it was about eastern religion they never really liked in the first place. The Judeo-Christian tradition, whatever else one might say about it, at least knew the weight of human suffering. When held against the torments of grief, loneliness, pain, disease, self-doubt and anxiety, the Maharishi's talk about "bliss consciousness" seemed romantic, even cheap. Perhaps the western teachings had shoved man down too far into a sense of incapacity and guilt, but was it any better to waft his ego into the pink clouds of "divinity?[1] "

As a measure of how seriously scientists take TM, over three hundred studies in some twenty nations have been conducted to date.[2] Of course the Maharishi's scientists claim validity for TM in the same manner that tobacco company scientists find little wrong with smoking. By and large, however, there is reason to suspect TM scientifically, as we will show.

It is felt that TM-produced data has been misused and exaggerated, much in the same way that the real purpose of TM has been concealed. Public relations motivation seems to guide the research of TM, and the results invariably follow the party line. But unbiased outside testing has provided some revelations.

Where subjective claims are made for TM (a "blissful feeling," an "alleviation of despair," etc.) they cannot really be tested. But TM has made a number of purely physiological claims in areas that are measurable and *can* be tested.

WHAT PRICE TM?

Transcendental Meditation does create physiological changes in its practicers; that much has been proven. It does have an effect. Exactly what causes the changes, however, the extent of the changes, their long-term effect, and whether, in fact, the changes are beneficial are matters still unsettled. So is the cost of the changes, in the sense of what the meditator might be giving up to effect them as he practices TM. We are aware, for instance, that a lobotomy calms a disturbed personality, but its ultimate cost is horrible. Morphine quiets the body at the expense of the brain. Any personality-modifying procedure has an attendant cost factor; such is the integration of the various psycho-physiological systems in human beings.

Selling one's soul to the devil has been a philosophical theme throughout man's literature; the seller's dreams come true for the moment, but the price must be ultimately paid, no matter how high. Jesus put it well: "What will it profit a man if he gain the whole world but lose his own soul?" The best technique possible for producing a perfectly integrated psycho-physiological human being will, when it becomes operational, have a cost factor. We will examine what benefits are available through TM in that light.

Also, we must consider, as we look into the data regarding a relatively new psychological procedure, that not much is firmly established. It might be fair to say that for every benefit of TM cited by a scientific proponent of the system, a scientist in the next village has been unable to verify it. Obviously we cannot cover all TM research in the available space, but we will summarize fairly the major claims, along with their evidence both for and against the procedure.

First of all, TM does make obvious bodily changes. It lowers the metabolism, including the heart rate, respiration and oxygen consumption; and increases alpha brain wave activity, which is primarily related to relaxation. These changes effect pleasant feelings in most meditators. Beyond these measurable changes, little is certain, and there is some dispute about these.[3] Reports of improved physiological and psychological functioning are based on individual subjective judgments and may well be related to TM-associated factors that have nothing to do with the meditation procedure, the mantra, the guru's ideals or anything else connected to TM. These factors may be related to changes in the meditator's life style that occur just because he is doing something new in his life.

Some individuals who come to TM are seekers—perhaps insecure, lonely, without a group to move in. TM, with its emphasis on cameraderie and support of the group, fills many needs. The group support, personal motivation, a sense of belonging to a movement, purpose, direction—all are factors of great impact. The assurances alone of many other meditators that a better life lies just ahead are enough to provide most initiates with a sense of well-being. Obviously the meditation itself has nothing to do with these ordinary social changes in the initiate's life style, for they could be caused as well by his joining any other group or movement.

Indeed, many other cults and sects based on religious or intellectual systems promise many of the same changes of life effected by TM. Scientology, Nichiren Shoshu, Self-Realization Fellowship and any number of other cultic societies report similar results to those of the TM experience. And obviously, since these groups are all basically opposed to each other and utilize entirely different philosophies and procedures, the group identification itself is principally responsible for the changes. Sometimes the mere introduction of a different daily regimen can make profound changes in certain personalities.

With that understood, we can examine the "Science has proven . . ." claims of TM cautiously. Caution becomes automatic because of the enormity of the claims if not because of the uniqueness of the subject.

The TM Book, a best-seller, gives almost wild promises to TM devotees, including improvement of one's intelligence, school grades, memory, reaction time, physical energy, personal relationships, productivity, job satisfaction, adaptability, personality stability, and on and on. On the physiological side, one may supposedly decrease one's blood pressure through practicing TM, conquer insomnia, asthma, anxiety and a host of other medical and psychological maladies. [4]

The book has been read by reliable scientists as well as by ordinary people looking for easy answers or a better life style. Harvard psychologist Gary Schwartz is skeptical:

> A lot of those charts are based on unpublished data which can be explained by many other reasons than those interpreted by the TM people. [5]

Dr. Schwartz suggests that the TM promoters simply promise more than they can deliver. [6]

Consultant neurophysiologist Dr. Peter Fenwick finds much fault with the TM research procedures, which he says are not up to the accepted standards of those normally utilized for such research outside of TM circles:

> All these studies need to be looked upon with reservations. Few include adequate control groups and none that I am aware of have yet used a blind control procedure where neither the subject nor observer is aware of the treatment given or the aims of the experiment. [7]

Dr. Fenwick says that until TM researchers adopt the standard procedures for accuracy, ''it is almost impossible to draw any conclusions.''

Research quality is invariably a problem whenever the researchers are promoters of the product being tested. We don't intend to cast doubt on every TM experiment, but obviously work handed in by meditators involved with the

TM organization and published by Maharishi International University Press and circulated by the TM organizations themselves is probably to be regarded as biased to some degree. Objectivity is most difficult to achieve with persons whose experimental results will either favor or condemn their own personal behavior. Harvard psychologist Dr. Dan Goleman noted a rather obvious peculiarity of TM research: ''Any follower of the research on TM notices that researchers who belong to the movement have never reported a negative finding.[8]''

Dr. Goleman laments that even M.D.s and psychiatrists have repeated the invalid scientific findings utilized by the TM organization in their books and publicity pamphlets. Many of the studies, he stated in the article, will probably never go through adequate scrutiny, though they remain powerfully persuasive ''scientific'' sales points for the program.[9]

Author John White, who has written numerous books on the general subject of altered consciousness, complains about the publicity value of imprecise conclusions. Under the chapter heading, ''The Scientific Case against TM,'' he says that if TM is effective just because of relaxation ''there seem to be a lot of scientists doing very poor research—research with results favorable to TM that is being hyped by SIMS.[10]''

Obviously, if there are never any negative results with TM experiments conducted by meditators themselves, we have either the ultimate panacea for all our ills that the guru has promised, or scientific objectivity is in question. An examination of the way the TM organization seems to handle its data is most revealing.

FIGURES DON'T LIE BUT . . . .

TM publications show a tendency to fail to tell the whole story scientifically. Studies are done, but the results reported tend to be less than candid, hiding sins of omission.

Drug abuse being the major problem that it is, TM promoters suggest that their system will decrease or even stop altogether the use of drugs. Several studies have been done which purport to show this, but as we shall see, the whole story is not told.

As a simple example of TM promoters' misuse of data, consider the research of Dr. Leon Otis, Director of Psychobiology and Physiology at the Stanford Research Institute. Dr. Otis concluded his studies with the suggestion that those who tend to give up drugs while on TM may do so more because of their personality structures than because of TM itself. He also noted that the cessation of drug usage typically occurred within the first three months of the program, and thus continued meditation had little to do with it.[11] But SIMS distributed over a million copies of a publicity booklet showing charts of Dr. Otis' findings which purported to prove that TM was responsible for the cessation and that the longer people meditate the less dependent they are upon drugs.

It is noteworthy to mention that the TM program requires its candidates to give up all non-prescription drugs for at least two weeks before they can receive their mantras. Thus, everyone who even begins the program has had to achieve cessation on his own. Obviously, every candidate who survives the initiation and begins meditating is *already* an easy drug quitter.

Then it is also noteworthy that TM is regarded by many people inside and outside of the program as a kind of "high" in itself. For some people it may well be just a kind of "replacement drug" rather than a way of getting off drugs.

The main study publicized by the TM organization to show that TM cuts drug abuse was one done by Dr. R.K. Wallace, a meditator, and Herbert Benson, M.D., an independent investigator. Dr. Benson has admitted that the study has several problems connected with it.[12] Indeed the results were less than dramatic; after twenty-one months of steady TM, thirty percent of the meditators were still on drugs.[13]

Dr. Otis, the Stanford researcher, pointed out in a paper delivered to the 1973 American Psychological Association that an average of five percent of those who had taken up TM *increased* their drug use.[14] Understandably, this latter study by Otis is not popular with the TM promoters, and does not appear in their findings. Investigation into skin resistance and anxiety levels by researcher Mike West of Cardiff University was published and promoted by the TM organization without his permission. While generally misrepresenting his findings, they also simply failed to report the negative data. West states:

> And if I had been asked I wouldn't have given permission, because just looking at the way they have reported the findings and the interpretation they have given them, it's a rather bad representation of the work I have done.[15]

In another example of the misuse of data, Maharishi International University put out a study purporting to show that TM leads to superior perceptual-motor performance, neglecting to include the experimenter's own notation, "The results are inconclusive.[16]"

Dr. Jack Sparks, who taught statistical psychology at Pennsylvania State University, examined five different studies on TM released by SIMS. Utilizing the original experimental reports in his study, Dr. Sparks found that three of the studies were listed by number (18, 41, 44) in *Fundamentals of Progress,* the main TM booklet backing the scientific claims for the program. Studies 18 and 41 each represented the *only* justification available for their claims, and Dr. Sparks began his procedure with these.

His results were discouraging in view of TM's claims. In one study (18) he found that no TM relationship could be demonstrated at all, and the conclusions of the other study were unwarranted from the data. Going on to yet other studies, he found that four out of the five experiments showed that nothing reliable could be concluded from the data. He noted in his conclusions that controls were generally nonexistent, sampling was erratic, and various changes recorded in individual subjects could not be specified as to whether they were or were not beneficial.[17]

Since the studies concerned rather crucial areas, one regrets that the TM investigators are not more reliable. Intelligence, neuroticism, prisoner rehabilitation and anxiety, and drug abuse were among the factors concerned.

There is perhaps a psychological effect working on the TM investigators themselves. The pressure to produce impressive results in TM studies seems to cause carelessness and misuse of data. The guru has clearly promised so much that the delivery is problematical. If TM were simply a way to relax or a beneficial technique for soothing anxieties, reliable experiments might possibly be forthcoming. But when it is supposed to solve all the problems of all the world, things go awry in the laboratory.

From the TM experiments it would seem scientifically justifiable only to conclude that sitting still with one's eyes closed for short periods each day is soothing.

SUPPOSE I TAKE A NAP INSTEAD?

There may be some justification for thinking that the mantra and all of the rest of the transcendental scene is just public relations. When one relaxes, one feels better.

A number of experimenters, at reputable universities and scientific laboratories, have not been able to back up basic claims of TM in subsequent studies. They have cast suspicion on the TM program and their conclusions make it appear to be only a fancy new packaging for ancient Hinduism. When the TM claims enter areas of measurable responses, testing them is easy. And here they generally fail to persuade.

Increased skin resistance is held by some to indicate reduced stress (though this is not clear), and studies conducted by TM promoters showed large increases in such skin resistance during meditation. Harvard University studies, however, could not verify the presence of the significant increased skin resistance during meditation.[18] *Psychology Today* rejected as "long ago proved faulty" the TM conclusion that lowered blood-lactate levels found in meditators indicated lessened anxiety.[19]

Dr. Otis and Dr. Sparks, both quoted above, seriously question TM's claims to have a positive effect in changing basic personality characteristics.[20] The criminal personality is supposed to be relaxed by TM, and the guru's organization went into quite an ambitious study of 240 American cities in this regard. Since the presence of one percent of meditators is supposed to affect the community and drop the crime rate, TM set out to find decreased crime rates in cities with this percentage. Indeed, the crime rate went down an average of eight percent in what the TM researchers called "one percent cities," and they found a nine percent crime increase in what they called non-meditating cities. The problem with such a study is the many variables involved in both meditation and crime. For example, several cities showing no demonstrable percentage of meditators showed a decreased crime rate also.[21]

While such statistics, based on large samplings, read very well in the TM promotional literature, it is good to remember that the data is not very specific. Crime rates increase and decrease according to myriads of social variables. Besides, where TM is concerned, it is very hard to know exactly how many people are really meditating in a given city or how exactly they are following the program. Crime rates vary according to what the local courts regard as crimes, and TM involvement varies with how effectively its public relations staff can inspire a community.

And finally, TM aside, it is possible that if certain criminal personalities are made to stop and rest twice a day they may be less active at their trades. Simple relaxation makes everybody feel better.

The heart rate and blood pressure variations in the process of TM are still unclear as to their ultimate effect. Little or no changes occur in the initial three months, whereas some effects show up at nine months or more.[22]

Regarding Maharishi's claim that TM is ''a natural and effective cure for mental illness,[23]'' Dr. John Donnelly, psychiatrist-in-chief of the four hundred-bed psychiatric hospital, the Institute of Living, in Hartford, Connecticut, undertook a three year TM project with his unusually large sampling of subjects. Dr. Donnelly's conclusion is plainly stated: ''Our findings did not indicate any significant difference in the treatment of psychiatric disorders.[24]''

The 1976 WGBH-TV production, ''Meditation and the Mind,'' presented the testimony of various scientific researchers of TM. Their work cast further doubt on numerous TM claims (e.g., improved memory, etc.), and they brought to light many of the problems associated with TM research. Dr. Peter Fenwick said: ''I think that we haven't found any evidence that TM is a separate state on the physiological level.'' The program, done with the advice and co-operation of the American Association for the Advancement of Science, queried: ''Much of the research on TM is done by meditators themselves and published in their own journals, which don't report contradictory results— why?'' The broadcast concluded near the end with the statement that ''scientific research and propaganda form an uneasy partnership.[25]''

It is becoming increasingly clear experimentally that TM may be just another name for simple ''unwinding'' and that what physiological relaxation changes do occur are not unique to the program although they tend to disappear when the program is stopped. Experimenter Dr. Benson, quoted above, says that TM and other such techniques will work only so long as they are employed daily. Moreover, he and others have duplicated all of the TM effects with similar procedures. Benson's own "relaxation response," which involves sitting quietly and meditating on the word "one," provides all the physiological effects of TM.[26] Like TM, it does not always work and can have undesirable side effects.[27] Other researchers have duplicated the TM effects by sitting quietly with the eyes closed, meditating on nothing in particular.[28] Dr. John Laragh, perhaps the leading expert on high blood pressure in the United States, says, "I'm not sure that meditating has any different effect on blood pressure than relaxing and sitting on a couch and reading a book.[29]"

The placebo effect of TM, the mere fact that relaxing of any sort has some beneficial effect on anybody, is held by many researchers to be more important that the meditation itself.

Dr. Jonathon Smith of the Psychology Department at Roosevelt University in Chicago believes that the therapeutic potential of TM is due to factors other than the TM practice itself: expectation of relief and the simple act of sitting with the eyes closed daily are the effective agents. "These findings support the conclusion that the critical therapeutic agent in TM is something other than the TM meditation exercise," he concludes.[30]

Dr. Otis and others have noted the crucial role played by simple expectancy in the TM effect. If one supposes the stuff will work, the stuff probably will work. This expectation of great things helps to define the experience as very beneficial before it is even undertaken by many people.[31]

Those who succeed in getting something out of TM, then, may be doing so for a number of reasons independent from the program itself: they may have predisposing personality factors toward that sort of relaxation program; they may enjoy the group support; they may be completely persuaded by the advance publicity about the beneficial effects; and so forth. Changes in some personalities may occur overnight simply by the decision to take up TM.[32] Some people get a lift out of making *any* decision, especially in the "self-help" area.

Obviously, if TM is just a placebo—a treatment that works because the client is convinced that it works—it is harmless. But unfortunately, as we shall see, TM comes imbued with all sorts of religious doctrine, postures of a philosophical kind unfamiliar to most western adherents, and a whole society of world-takeover types of promoters. The initiate is swept into more than a relaxation exercise with TM. He becomes part of an international movement aimed at instilling a new (or very old) philosophy into the global community. We will examine the religious and philosophical implications of this "placebo" in the next chapter.

BUT DOES IT MAKE YOU SMART?

Non-physiological benefits, such as increased creativity, educational help, and so forth, are claimed for TM. These are a bit more difficult to measure than the bodily effects, but they have been examined in non-partisan circles with discouraging results for TM.

Some investigators feel that TM leads to *decreased* creative activity, since creativity is a function of a mentally stimulating environment and TM seeks to reach a void of mental stimulation. The meditator goes after peace in the sense of the temporary absence of active thinking, whereas the learning process seems to operate best in the presence of energetic thinking.

Dr. Colin Martindale, Harvard professor, feels that TM, biofeedback and other such methods "may have the side effect of decreasing our ability to think creatively.[33]" Dr. Martindale cites the fact that creative people typically show many spontaneous fluctuations in their skin conductance, while TM meditators show very few. Dr. Gary Schwartz, quoted above, undertook actual creativity test batteries, trying meditators against non-meditators, and noted that, "The meditators did consistently worse" on some scales and scored no better than non-meditators over all.[34] Dr. Schwartz theorizes that too much TM may interfere with the brain's capacity for logical, step-by-step thinking.

Where children are concerned, TM could be very detrimental. The TM organizations like to court the school systems as a way of integrating their program into the whole fabric of a given society, but TM may retard the all-important initial learning processes of the early years. Mary Rainey, a specialist in perception programs and a doctoral candidate at Stanford University in Early Childhood Education, is very much opposed to the use of TM as an educational tool with children. She feels that TM is a superficial and short-lived educational method, at best, and an incomplete learning process that does not give the child a definite frame of reference, but only freedom without responsibility.[35] Moral boundaries blur in TM.

A simple comparison of the results of western and eastern educational methods leaves little doubt that the west, with its methodical, step-by-step learning processes, has achieved more than the east with its typical passive meditative processes. In the simplest terms, the western work-at-it method of problem solving appears incomparably more successful when compared to the eastern meditate-on-it. All of the cave sitting and philosophizing of Hindu history has not proved able even to feed the people of India, despite its interesting contribution to world literature and culture. The musing of sages is a luxury to be afforded by those who have first solved the problems of living with nature for the common good.

PANNING THE PANACEA

It appears, then, that TM is not all Maharishi says it is, at least scientifically speaking. We will go more deeply into what TM really does and really is in the next two chapters, but to wrap up our scientific experiment survey we might conclude that TM is objectively nothing much.

It does have a psycho-physiological effect upon an individual, but this might well be attributed to TM-related causes rather than to TM itself. It is not a cure for anything, it does not help creativity and it does not really solve problems. It is at best a way of dealing with certain ordinary symptoms of modern life such as tension, alienation, but it does not treat or affect in any way the underlying causes.

It does not really appeal to so many people over the long run, as witnessed by its 25-50% drop-out rate,[36] and it does not even vaguely begin to justify its claims to be a global panacea.

Its scientific research, published by Maharishi International University under sober titles ("Scientific Research on Transcendental Meditation: Collected Papers") does not answer to independent, carefully controlled studies and experiments, and much of its charisma is just that and no more.

As to the possibility that TM appeals to and helps *some* people in some way, there is a price involved. Hindu God-Realization, which we will discuss next, does certainly have a profound effect on those who undertake it, as do most religious systems.

For those who persist in this meditation there are dangers, which we mean to make clear, and personality changes that they may eventually abhor. Spiritually, disastrous results may be obtained from TM.

The guru's system is, in a scientific sense, a lot less than he promises. But in a dangerous, subjective spiritual sense, it is far more.

FOOTNOTES: CHAPTER TWO

Introductory quotes: *Inauguration of the Dawn of the Age of Enlightenment*, p. 55; *Everything You Want to Know About TM*, p. 144; *Transcendental Medication*, p. 99; *The Seven States of Consciousness*, p. 163; *On the Bhagavad Gita*, p. 73; (Bombay: C.D. Taraporevala & Sons, 1960), 4th ed., p. 30.

1. *The New Religions* (Doubleday, 1970), pp. 134-5.

2. White, *Everything You Want to Know About TM* (Pocket, 1976), p. 52.

3. "Meditation and the Mind," WGBH-TV production, 125 Western Avenue, Boston, Mass. 02134, Nova #303, transcript, 1976.

4. Denniston and McWilliams, (Warner, 1975).

5. *Time*, August 25, 1975.

6. *Psychology Today*, April 1974, p. 39.

7. *The London Times Education Supplement*, May 17, 1974.

8. *Psychology Today*, Nov. 1975, p. 91.

9. *Ibid.*

10. White, *op. cit.*, p. 62.

11. *The Psychobiology of Meditation: Some Psychological Changes*, pp. 14-16, Chart 20, (Menlo Park, CA 94025: Stanford Research Institute); White, *op. cit.*, p. 56; *Psychology Today*, Aug. 1974, p. 46.

12. Herbert Benson, *The Relaxation Response* (William and Morrow, 1975), pp. 107-8.

13. Bloomfield, *op. cit.*, chart 21; cfa Una Kroll, *The Healing Potential of Transcendental Meditation* (John Knox 1974), p. 66.

14. Otis, *op. cit.*, p. 16, chart 22.

15. "Meditation and the Mind," see Note 3 above.

16. Denniston, pp. 4, 158, with *The Psychobiology of Transcendental Meditation: A Literature Review*, The final report of the Stanford Research Institute by Demetri Kanellakos, Jerome Lukas, p. 63; MIU Press pamphlet, *Scientific Research on Transcendental Meditation*, Chart 11; cf. *The Atlantic Monthly*, Oct. 1975, p. 39.

17. Research conducted for Spiritual Counterfeits Project, P.O. Box 4308, Berkeley, CA 94704, partially published in *Right On*, Nov. 1975, p. 10.

18. *Psychology Today*, April 1974, p. 40.

19. *Ibid.*, Nov. 1975, p. 91

20. Sparks, *op. cit.*; Otis, *op. cit.*, pp. 10, 12.

21. Forem, *Transcendental Meditation*, p. 254.

22. Jerome S. Lukas, "The Effects of TM on Concurrent Heart Rate, Peripheral Blood Pulse Volume, and the Alpha Wave Frequency," from the Stanford Research Institute, Menlo Park, CA; the final SRI report (Note 16), p. 66, "The Psychophysiology of Transcendental Meditation—A Pilot Study;" Jodi Lawrence, *Alpha Brainwaves* (Avon, 1972), p. 174; Claudio Naranjo & Robert Ornstein, *On the Psychology of Meditation* (Viking Press, 1974), p. 216.

23. Maharishi, *Transcendental Meditation*, p. 191.

24. White, *op. cit.*, p. 63.

25. Transcript obtained from WGBH-TV, 125 Western Avenue, Boston, Massachusetts, 02134, Nova #303. cf. L.S. Otis, "TM and Sleep," which also raises doubts about the uniqueness of the TM state (Stanford Research Institute).

26. *New York Times*, Feb. 9, 1975; Benson, *op. cit.*, pp. 68, 122; *Psychology Today*, April 1974, p. 40; "Meditation and the Mind," see Note 3.

27. Benson, *op. cit.*, pp. 109, 121.

28. White, *op. cit.*, pp. 56-60, 63; Otis, *op. cit.*, p. 14; see Note 3.

29. *Time*, Oct. 13, 1975.

30. White, *op. cit.*, p. 58.

31. *Ibid.*, p. 60; *Psychology Today*, November 1975, p. 91.

32. Otis, *op. cit.*, p. 6.

33. *Psychology Today*, July, 1975, p. 50.

34. *Psychology Today*, April, 1974, p. 43.

35. Douglas Shah, *The Meditators* (Logos, 1975), pp. 40-44.

36. *Time*, Oct. 13, 1975; Otis, *op. cit.*, p. 15; testimony of ex-teacher Greg Randolph in taped interview from SCP, Box 4308, Berkeley, CA 94704.

"Well, LSD is Western Yoga. The aim of all Eastern religion, like the aim of LSD, is basically to get high: that is, to expand your consciousness and find ecstasy and revelation within."

—Timothy Leary

"The holy tradition of great masters . . . is not merely held in high regard, but has come to be actually worshipped by seekers of truth and knowers of Reality."
—Maharishi Mahesh Yogi

"In view of the overwhelming evidence of the religious nature of TM as found in the English translation of the Vedic chant and in the actual meanings of the mantras assigned to those who join the movement, in view of the continued insistence upon secrecy by TM officials, and in view of the movement's growing number of legal entanglements, it is my contention that no further government support of any kind should be provided and that whatever has been granted, in local, state or federal programs, should be withdrawn."
—Robert Brank Fulton (Yale Ph.D.)

"A corpse is selected . . . [and] the Devata [god] materializes by means of the corpse. There is possession of it (Avesa)—that is, the entry of the Devata into the dead body. At the conclusion of a successful rite, . . . the head of the corpse turns round, and, facing the Sadhaka (yogi), speaks, bidding him name his boon, which may be spiritual or worldly advancement as he wishes. This [rite] is . . . attended by many terrors."
—Tantric yoga ritual

"When the cause of bondage is removed, the yogi can . . . enter into any living or dead body, and thus fulfill its past karma."

—Shree Purohit Swami

"It is a hazardous leap, no doubt—the final plunge into the deepest abyss of that Being which is identical with Nonbeing."

—Haridas Chaudhuri

CHAPTER THREE

THAT OLD-TIME RELIGION

Make no mistake about it—TM is Hinduism to the core.

In origin, initiation rites, practice and theory, Transcendental Meditation is Hinduism, and that's all there is to that. It is not advertised or sold that way, but is deceptively presented as some new, present-day discovery.

It is very easy to show that TM is Hinduism, pure and simple, just as its master is a Hindu.

That in itself does not make TM in any way bad to many people. However, as we will show throughout this book, there are spiritual dangers involved in the practice of this occult religion. Most people undertaking TM are not courted in the Hindu way and haven't a notion of what they are getting into. But both authors have experienced something of this Hindu scene personally, have gathered much ''secret'' material, and can report accurately on the total effects of this meditation system. John Weldon went through the actual TM *puja*, or initiation rite; Zola Levitt studied with a Yoga master and performed physical exercise, meditation, and study of *koans* (the "mind-murdering" riddles of Zen).

The originators of TM, historically—Shankara, Guru Dev and Maharishi—all belong to the Vedanta School of Hinduism, and this is what they promote. Despite any claims to the contrary, the meditation they teach cannot be, and is not, removed from its Hindu roots. The main purpose of the meditation itself is Hinduism's "God Realization," or the recognition of one's own deity. "Everybody is part of Brahman, the Impersonal Absolute of Hinduism," goes the party line. The recognition and understanding of this principle is the whole purpose of TM. Meditation leads the meditator into a new realization of the "oneness" of the universe, in the pantheistic way (everything is God).

This achievement is but one step in the forbiddingly complex hierarchy of states of consciousness. Cosmic Consciousness, a higher TM state, takes about five years to achieve and involves the steady, twenty-four hours per day realization of oneness with Brahman. Maharishi regards this state of consciousness as greatly rewarding and describes it thus: "Everything is Brahman (to) the performer who is established in Cosmic Consciousness," and "Brahman is the state of Cosmic Consciousness.[1]"

A look at Hindu thought in general is necessary if we are to understand Maharishi's purpose in spreading TM.

REALITY IS NOT REALITY

What we see is not what we get in Hinduism. Brahman is the only reality and everything else is delusion and dreams.

The stuff we perceive around us, says this philosophy, has a type of existence, like dreams have a type of existence, but is ultimately unreal. Reality, in reality, is not reality. people, nature, the world, the universe, are all just a dream—or at least what we perceive of those things with our senses is just a dream. Behind everything is Brahman, the only *real* reality.

Man is composed of two parts, in this thinking. There is one self—his body, his personality—which is not truly real. Then there is his true Self, which is in unity with Brahman, even though he doesn't yet realize it. That latter Self is the one which perceives *real* reality. The former self is deluded and in bondage to what it mistakenly perceives around it—the world, the suffering and the problems of life. It is as if we see through a distorting lens. Until we realize our oneness with Brahman, we operate by pure misinformation.

This is somewhat similar to Christian doctrine, where an accurate knowledge of God solves a faulty perception of the world. However, the vital difference involves what sort of ''god'' we seek to know. Brahman, unlike God, is indescribable, unmanifested, and reachable only by annihilation of logical thinking processes—a deadening of the mind as in TM, rather than a renewing of the mind as in the Gospel. When experienced Hindu masters attempt to apprehend Brahman, and to describe it, their descriptions leave us wondering again. (Maharishi: ''Brahman, which is an all pervading mass of bliss, does not exhibit any quality of bliss.[2]'')

The elusive Brahman is said to be nowhere yet everywhere; absolute, but relative; eternally immutable, yet ever-changing. Brahman solves a lot of problems, once It is tracked down, but as gods go It is certainly hard to communicate with.

TM's Cosmic Consciousness is supposed, by Maharishi, to be the perfect means of achieving oneness with Brahman once and for all. This modern guru agrees with Krishna (one of Vishnu's incarnations) that Cosmic Consciousness ''is the state of Brahman . . . having attained it, a man is not deluded.[3]'' But this involves some five years of meditation, on the average, as we pointed out. One would have to be extremely frustrated by the world and its problems to go this entire route to find "real reality."

The road to the Hindu heaven seems to be paved with incomprehensible contradictions. Indeed, the "Perfect Masters" delight in boggling the mind with such contradictions. The very idea of dulling the mind with a repeated mantra in order to sharpen the mind to a new view of reality leaves most people mystified. But the contradictions themselves and the seeming pointlessness of it all are considered useful exercise for minds that have become bogged down in misconceptions of reality. Mind-bending contradictions are cleansing to minds dirtied up with illusions about reality, goes this thinking.

An example of one of the *koans* posed to co-author Zola Levitt in his study of Yoga under a Master might help to explain the process of cleansing the mind through filling it with absurdity. Levitt had achieved meditation in the lotus position for 30 minutes each dawn (a simply killing exercise to anyone who, mistakenly or otherwise, perceives that his legs aren't made to bend that way) and was considered ready for mental exercises. The first problem posed by the Master was:

There is a portrait of a man with a beard. A Master looks at the portrait and says, "Why doesn't that man wear a beard?"

That's all. No information is supplied as to what the question is, what is to be done with the situation, or what it is for. The Master would reply, "I don't know," to any question about the *koan*.

"I was placed in a small room for twenty minutes to meditate about the portrait situation," recalls Levitt.

"I assumed that the question to be solved was why the Master thought the man in the portrait did *not* have a beard, even though it was specified that he did. After about 30 seconds I was tired of trying to solve this absurdity. My best answer was that the Master was a blind man. But my own

Master had said that many solutions would come to a good meditator, so I buckled down and reviewed the whole problem again. My Master had said that there were many levels of perception in the mind and new answers would continually come through meditation.

"He was right. I began to develop new answers as I concentrated, trying desperately to reason out this unreasonable problem. Perhaps the Master was commenting on painting in general—that painting was not real, and should never be taken as real. Perhaps he was saying that all life is like a portrait, subject to some artist's interpretation and totally unreal. Or maybe he was even admitting his own faulty perception of things and saying clearly that he could not trust his senses to accurately perceive a portrait.

"As the twenty minutes sped by—and they truly sped by—I was utterly fascinated by the exercise—I began to put all my conclusions together into a satisfactory picture of what really happened when the master encountered the portrait.

"This was my best and final answer: the Master in the *koan* was a man who had long ago achieved oneness with Brahman and was thus never deluded. What he was doing was instructing all students present that it is better to assume the opposite of what one sees. The artist's eye interpreted the subject of the portrait to begin with. Perhaps he saw a beard where there was none—there's a small chance of that. When the artist's hand moved the brush over the canvas, perhaps it painted a beard mistakenly—there's a small chance of that, too. The portrait may have changed as life went on and the sun rose and fell and the air brushed by the canvas through the years—there's a very small chance of that. Then the Master came, undeluded but looking at a worldly (illusory) portrait. Perhaps even his experienced eye was party to the unrelenting unreality all around us—there's a small chance of that. Finally, we have the Master's remark, possibly faultily heard by his listeners, or faultily presented to me by my own Master, or faultily heard by me.

"On the deepest level I began to realize that my own thinking process might be faulty, too, and that the problem was not at all what I was solving. Was the room really there around me? After all, my mind was off in that fictional room where the portrait hung. Was I solving the problem or was I dreaming about solving the problem? Was my Master going to be there after the twenty minutes? What is twenty minutes? Would I open that door and confront Brahman instead of my Master? Was my Master Brahman? Was *I* Brahman?

"On a still deeper level I began to reason, 'I'm going nuts, thinking like this (which was possible). But I'm intrigued. My Master is right—reality is not reality.'

"In any case, I opened the door in twenty minutes, found my Master and presented my answer to the *koan*. I stated with brevity, in the traditional lingo, 'Reality is not reality,' and waited for my Master's response. I thought I had done quite well.

"His response was, as always, 'I don't know.' "

There is much more to Hinduism, and transcendental meditation than problem solving, of course, but the above may give a picture of how the mind is exercised through what westerners would call "mind-boggling" situations. Admittedly co-author Levitt found deeper levels of consciousness, for want of a better term, through the exercise. But as to whether they were beneficial, whether they in fact led any closer to Brahman, or whether Brahman is worth finding at all, are still open questions.

Jesus often spoke in parables to the crowds who listened to His teachings, and these have been pondered for nearly 2,000 years in the west, with some disagreement as to their ultimate meaning. The contemplation of God is not at all exclusive to the Hindu faith; but the attempt to subtly convert the unsuspecting to a new "god" is something else. Christians, for example, when speaking of Christ, are eager to expose all that they know about their Master and frankly to share everything the Bible says in order that the initiate may accurately contemplate the nature of God. The TM teachers, as we shall presently see, indoctrinate others with their religion by shrewdly camouflaging it with non-religious concepts acceptable to westerners. They conceal their god until the initiate is prepared for the process of receiving him.

Maharishi's own definition of his god and his explanation of how to get to him through TM leaves one begging for more clarity and precision.

> The practice of transcendental meditation purifies the intellect . . . (to perceive) that you are that Reality which you have gained during meditation, Transcendental Consciousness, you are That and all this is That, and That alone is and all this is nothing, immediately the man gains unity, consciousness of unity in life in the midst of all diversity. [4]

The only thing that is clear is that TM is unclear, and Brahman is unclear. It is up to the initiate to be fascinated enough to pursue Maharishi's ideas to their ultimate promised fulfillment.

It should be said that we cannot hope to define Hinduism, or any other philosophical system, in this space, but we have tried to stick to quotations and personal experiences to explain the essentials. What we have said will serve our purposes of exposing the religious side of TM and how its salesmen conceal it.

HINDUS? WHO, US!?

The true spiritual nature of TM—that it is in fact Hinduism—is kept out of the advertising. Eastern religion has never had very many customers in the west and that's not the way to sell TM over here. Only when the movement gathers irresistible momentum will its purveyors begin to admit the truth about it.

Ex-TM teachers, some of whom are interviewed in Chapter Seven, have disclosed that there *is* a plan to call a spade a spade in the TM publicity, but only if things go according to schedule. Charles Lutes, president of the Spiritual Regeneration Movement, indicated on July 19, 1975, that there was a cover-up:

> The popularization of the movement in non-spiritual terms was strictly for the purpose of gaining the attention of people who wouldn't have paid the movement much mind if it had been put in spiritual terms. [5]

Lutes went on to point out that it didn't much matter what reason an initiate had for starting TM—he would eventually get to the spiritual side of it. Such is the nature of the meditation, Lutes said, that the end result is invariably spiritual. Thus, if one approaches TM just for curiosity or for relief from physical tension, one will end up seeking Brahman if all goes according to plan.

Jhan Robbins and Dave Fisher, both meditators and authors of *Tranquility Without Pills: All About Transcendental Meditation,* cited a meditator who discovered that "almost inevitably meditators look to the Supreme Being (Brahman).[6]"

Maharishi himself vacillates between admitting to the religious side of his system and concealing that information for the sake of higher membership roles. He writes, "God realization has been said to be the aim of life,[7]" and again, "Transcendental deep meditation is a way to consciously arrive at the state of the impersonal transcendental absolute Being, the almighty transcendental God.[8]" But in more of a public relations frame of mind he candidly observed, "Not in the name of God-realization can we call a man to meditate in the world of today, but in the name of enjoying the world better, sleeping well at night, being wide awake during the day.[9]"

Perhaps the Master, a devout man in his way, is merely lamenting modern man's godlessness, in which he would be joined by many a western clergyman. But then it seems rather deceptive to promise a method for "enjoying the world better" through a system which teaches that the world is not really there at all. The guru seems too ready to compromise his own beliefs in order to gather followers.

True enough, most westerners would be turned off by a $125 way to arrive at "Being," "The Source of All Thought," "Pure Creative Intelligence," and all the rest of the easternisms. Mumbo jumbo is mumbo jumbo, and watchers of TV commercials, to say nothing of TM commercials, are wary of it. But in Maharishi's books many statements of his faith and its connection to TM are revealed. "The Incarnation of Lord Krishna," praises to Brahman, "hymns of the Vedas and Bhagavad-Gita" and the equating of Brahman *with* Being come up in Maharishi's TM textbooks.[10] The four texts to be utilized by meditators encompass over 1,000 pages and clearly document the religious nature of the guru's system of meditation as well as his personal adherence to Hinduism.

We do not object to the guru following his faith, of course. His spiritual position is up to him. Where we must object is in the rather successful touting of TM as some kind of scientifically verified, non-religious cure for all ills. Either the guru is trying to spread his Hinduistic faith, or he's not. The truth is carefully hidden from the casual observer of the ads and posters, as well as from the initiate into the program itself.

Maharishi's intentions, however, which are pursued by all of the TM organizations, are quite clear to unbiased investigators. Now that we have defined the Master's real spiritual posture, and given a brief definition of the sort of Hinduism he advocates, we can go on to document in depth the fact that TM is religious.

It should be understood that TM proponents everywhere almost invariably disclaim any religious connection. Robbins and Fisher state flatly in their TM book, "Teachers of the TM movement are quick to point out that their technique is not in any way similar to a religion." Asked the question, "Is TM a religion?" Robbins and Fisher replied, "No. Everyone involved in the practice of TM emphasizes that. Although TM does stem from Eastern religious tradition, it is not a religion and has absolutely no religious overtones.[11]"

The TM Book says, "The TM program does not involve any religious belief or practice—Hindu or otherwise.[12]" Jack Forem, TM author and New York area Coordinator for SIMS says, "The TM program is not a philosophy or a religion, but a practical technique.[13]" He says of Maharishi, "He emphasized that he was not espousing philosophy or religion, or offering something to believe in or accept on faith.[14]" *Time* magazine quoted the guru as asserting, "We are not a religion.[15]" The TM information booklets published by the Spiritual Regeneration Movement contain, like a formula, the repeated statement, "TM is not a religion."

We still say TM *is* a religion.

SPEAK FOR YOURSELF, JOHN

Co-author John Weldon will never believe TM is not a religion, especially after he bowed low beside his offerings of fresh fruit, flowers and a clean white handkerchief at his own initiation into TM.

"When I decided that I wanted to be initiated into TM," John recalls, "I was informed about the *puja*, or initiation ceremony, and told that I would be given my mantra at that ceremony. I was to bring the specified items as an offering. Nor could I refuse the initiation rite. Anyone who refuses does not get a mantra and thus cannot meditate in the TM way.

"I was told to remove my shoes before entering the TM initiation room. Inside was a picture of Guru Dev, Maharishi's late Master, hanging over a makeshift altar. My instructor informed me that this was 'a very holy ceremony.'

61

"I stood by while my instructor began chanting in sanskrit. There was no translation and I had no idea what he was saying. (See translation in appendix.) At the end of his prayer my instructor bowed low before the altar and bade me do the same. I did so.

"He then gave me my mantra (ieng) with instruction on how to pronounce it. I was told to go off and meditate on my mantra for fifteen minutes, then to return to be checked on how I was doing.

"It struck me, through all of this, that I was not simply a witness to a religious ceremony, but an active participant. Naturally the chanting in the strange tongue had an effect on me. I later realized that the atmosphere was meant to appeal to my spiritual side. I did have that effect at the time.

"I was directly involved in bringing my offerings, removing my shoes in the eastern religious tradition, and bowing down before the altar and picture of Guru Dev. It was in my kneeling position before the honored guru that I received my mantra; and it was not lost on me that I owed the creation of my mantra to the dead guru. I have since reflected with amazement upon TM organization statements to the effect that the initiate is not involved in the initiation ceremony but only observes it.

"Upon learning the translation of the *puja*, I fully realized just how religious a ceremony I had been made to take part in. And when I encountered the Pledge to Maharishi that all TM teachers must sign, I realized how deceptive the religious disclaimers were. Having pledged his faithfulness in 'spreading the light of God to all those who need it,' my instructor knew very well that he was pronouncing a religious rite over an unknowing convert.

"Like all other initiates, I had been subtly drawn into Hinduism without my knowledge, under the cover of a foreign language and the deceptive promise that 'TM is not a religion.'

JUDGE FOR YOURSELF

We reproduce below a comparison of statements by leading Maharishi International University spokesmen with a portion of the translated *puja* as chanted by the TM instructor in initiation ceremonies. The full text of the *puja* is given at the end of this chapter.

MIU FACULTY STATEMENTS

"TM . . . is not a religious practice. It doesn't require faith and it doesn't require worship.16 "

—Seymour Migdal,
Dean of Faculty,
MIU

"First of all, the person learning the TM technique doesn't involve himself in the ceremony at all, he merely witnesses it. Secondly, as any teacher of the TM technique will tell you, it is not a religious ceremony at all. In no way does it involve religious belief, or even any belief at all.17 "

—Jonathon Shear,
Prof. of Philosophy,
MIU

PUJA

"To LORD NARAYANA, to lotus-born BRAHMA the Creator to . . . GOVINDA, ruler among the yogis . . . to SHANKARACHARYA the redeemer, hailed as KRISHNA and BADARAYANA, to the commentator of the BRAHMA SUTRAS I bow down. To the glory of the LORD I bow down again and again, at whose door the whole galaxy of gods pray for perfection day and night . . . GURU (i.e., Guru Dev) in the glory of BRAHMA, GURU in the glory of the great LORD SHIVA, GURU in the glory of the personified transcendental fullness of BRAHMAN, to Him, to SHRI GURU DEV adorned with glory, I bow down.[18] "

In this ceremony the three main Hindu gods, Brahma, Vishnu and Shiva, are actually worshipped in the person of Guru Dev. As the initiate stands dumbfounded at his own initiation, his trusted instructor rattles off the names and titles of Hindu deities and sages and makes him a partner in their worship, while the very professors at the organization's own university deny the whole religious afffair.

Something is rotten in Delhi.

Guru Dev is referred to in the *puja* as "His Divinity," being an "Ascended Master," while Guru Maharishi himself enjoys the lesser title of "His Holiness" because Maharishi is still alive. Dev has attained divinity by virtue of death, which apparently is the current TM Master's future honor as well.

THE OLD RUGGED *BHAJANA*

Not only is the TM initiation rite strictly religious, but Maharishi hasn't even bothered to change it from the standard Hindu *pujas* of the past. The TM initiation ceremony follows the traditional format of worship used in Hinduism for ages—with the difference that the real Hindus at least understood the religious nature of their own ceremony.

Ernest Wood, former Dean of the American Academy of Asian Studies, points out that "The Hindus have collective, though not organized, worship, in the form of *bhajanas,* in which songs are sung, containing mostly the names of the deities . . . before a statue or a picture representing the divinity.[19] " T.J. Hopkins, in his *The Hindu Religious Tradition* notes that the Hindu *puja* is characterized by the invoking of the deity, an extended series of offerings to the deity, praise and worship of the deity, and a representation or image of the deity.

Guru Dev's picture is no accident at TM initiation ceremonies, of course, and it means more than just respect for the former Master. As Hopkins comments, "The image in *puja* is treated as one would treat the god himself in person, for the image *is* the god in person: it is his *murti*, his 'form' made manifest for his worshippers. This sense of the deity as a person and the image as his representative form is fundamental to the meaning of *puja* and is always preserved in *puja* rituals.[20]"

Before this picture, then, the initiate is made to bow and present his offerings in this "non-religious" ceremony.

The old rugged *bhajana* is something to be reckoned with, and not just in its religious sense. It has been arranged through trial and error over the millennia, to have the optimum psychological effect on the initiates in its sequence of sounds and its obvious "sanctity." The TM *puja* itself is really one long mantra designed and calculated to produce an altered state of consciousness, which can be induced by the chanting of certain musical rhythms, and often is.

This is the sinister side of the TM initiation rites. The unwary initiate is placed in a passive, receptive frame of mind suitable to the *deep* implantation of his mantra in the brain. TM utilizes the *bija* mantras, or "seed" mantras. As a seed is pushed into the ground, so the mantra is imbedded into the mind of the initiate. The TM instructor knows and feels a lot more than he is saying in the rite. It is believed that his very recitation of the *puja* "tunes him in" to Maharishi and the rest of the hierarchy of dead Masters, supplying psychic power to the teacher for the implantation.

The Puja Commentary gives the details of this psychic trick played on the initiate, in the laudable language of his being done a great favor. How much disservice he is actually being done is unclear, but that the process is deceptive is obvious.

When the manipulation of human minds is called "brain-washing," people get up in arms about it. When it is called TM, it becomes a happy new fad.

But then, those who brainwash sometimes admit it.

GOD, PRAYER, FAITH AND TM

So much for the initiation rite. It is a religious ceremony, complete with obeisance, offerings and even a calculated religious-psychological effect upon the initiate.

We find that the rest of TM—the actual practice of the meditation—is also a thoroughly religious endeavor. There is no way to separate the practice of TM from its religion.

Experienced TM meditators and the movement's leaders make the usual non-religious claims for the TM procedure, but this runs counter to their announced world goals. The seventh goal of the TM World Plan is "To achieve the spiritual goals of mankind in this generation.[21] " Charles Lutes, president of SRM states, "It was in Madras, in 1958, that Maharishi came to the resolve to dedicate his life to the limitless goal of the spiritual regeneration of the world.[22] " The quote appears in the preface of Maharishi's definitive work, *Transcendental Meditation.*

What is spiritual regeneration according to Maharishi? It involves classical Hinduism's God-Realization concept, as we have seen—getting virtually everyone to meditate and to experience Brahman, the Absolute.

Now the guru is worldly-wise enough, as we have seen, not to broadcast his religious message too obviously. He seldom preaches any sort of doctrine when talking about TM, especially when talking with the secular American media. Once in a while someone inquires if he is not down-playing this central aspect of his system. He was frank enough to tell the San Francisco *Chronicle* (March 29, 1975), "I'm not downplaying it. It's only that I'm not talking about it."

Whatever the guru happens to be talking about at any given time, for any selected purpose, *it is still very important to realize that the TM goal and Brahman-realization are equivalent.* One cannot meditate in the prescribed manner of TM without absorbing into his life eventually the inevitable effects of yoga. The Hindu experience is the Hindu experience, whether described as TM or described in the mumbo jumbo of the clan.

Recently *Education Digest* and *Church and State* ran TM articles concluding that Maharishi's theories were "pure Hindu theology." But they mistakenly commented, "TM may be going to school, but Hindu theology and ritual will have to remain off the school grounds.[22a]" Both apparently failing to understand that TM *alone and of itself* is Hinduism because of its designed effect. Hindu God-realization, "creative intelligence" and all the other "scientific" terms describing the TM goal are simply disguised equivalents for Brahman.

One is reminded of the LSD tests conducted on unknowing subjects by governmental agencies. It seems too obvious to point out that the subjects were equally drugged, and with disastrous results, whether they knew they were taking the hallucinogen or were convinced they were ingesting ordinary substances. The calculated, purposeful effect of TM is there, whether the meditator is aware of it or not, and whether the guru speaks of it or not.

The substitution of pseudo-scientific terms for the relevant Hindu terms in TM has the effect of placing the meditator in an unguarded position, but the stuff works nevertheless. One does not achieve "simple mental relaxation" with TM; one achieves the realization of Brahman, but in the names of "creative intelligence" and "pure awareness."

Maharishi's private statements, in his books and other written materials, are much more revealing on the religious nature of the TM experience than are his public statements, as we would expect. "It is because the Self is joined in Union with Brahman that a man enjoys eternal happiness," asserts the guru frankly in his commentary, *On the Bhagavad Gita*,[23] Maharishi obviously does not think TM is anything new, and does not claim to have invented a new system with a new effect. As a yogi, he has merely designed a new packaging for an old product which he feels is still worth selling.

In connection with TM, Maharishi speaks freely of God, prayer and faith, essentials of all religions, even while his publicity agents omit these volatile terms. "The path to God realization is this meditation. Transcendental Meditation is a path to God," he says, giving his PR people a few head-aches.[24] TM is "a very good form of prayer . . . a most refined and most powerful form of prayer is this meditation which directly leads us to the field of the Creator, to the sources of Creation, to the field of God.[25]" Latching on to prayer, a most respected concept for reaching God through-out the world, the Master is assuming a sort of religious endorsement for TM. Who can have anything against prayer? And perhaps TM provides a more effective, more up-to-date way to pray, think the consumers, especially after they look at the guru's "scientific evidence."

Faith is a more murky concept than prayer. Almost every-body has faith in something. Even to purely secular man, faith is a bolstering PR word. People *like* faith. Faith makes everyone feel good.

But talk about faith can backfire. Those already practicing a genuine religious faith are not looking for any replace-ments, and are quick to reject new and unfamiliar faith systems. So we again end up with a double PR effect, causing the officials of the various agencies to avoid using the word faith, while the guru touts it in his personal writings. With all of the denials about faith that are seen in the TM pamphlets, the Master still goes on connecting his brainchild meditation system with faith: "Moreover the experience of transcendental meditation is such that it can be started from whatever level of faith a man may have, for it brings faith to the faithless . . . .26 ' Maharishi feels that TM "causes faith to grow." This is the great benefit of TM to humanity, because "for the ultimate fulfillment in God-consciousness the greatest faith is needed.27 "

TM teachers need great faith in the system, counsels the guru, in order to progress successfully. Ex-teachers report that the Master urged great faith on the part of progressing meditators as they passed through the three TM states (transcendental, cosmic, and God-consciousness) "As the mind passes through all these states, it has to undergo various new experiences which, in the absence of faith, can easily be misunderstood at any step. That is why the Lord (Krishna) names faith as a prerequisite to knowledge.28 "

Since the light of this knowledge is kindled in one who is "full of faith, 29 " those without faith can be in serious trouble. Ex-teachers have specified that reaching TM's state of Cosmic consciousness can provide the agonizing experience of convincing the meditator that he has lost his mind. It is essential at that point for a more experienced meditator to explain the transition in terms of a normal extension of faith, not insanity. But in some cases insanity *is* the result. More on that below.

The very essence of most religions—salvation, sanctification, immortality—is also a part of TM, according to Maharishi, who does not shrink from making these claims for his system. The guru says that the Vedas, the sacred Hindu writings which are the source of TM, lead man to salvation. "Having gained the state of Brahman, a man has risen to the ultimate Reality of existence. In this state of enlightenment he has accomplished eternal liberation . . .30 " Immortality, salvation, God's will, sanctification—TM is integrally related to them all, according to the Master.31

He wraps up his spiritual evaluation of TM in all-embracing religious terms:

> The key to fulfillment of every religion is found in the regular practice of transcendental deep meditation. [32]

TELLING IT LIKE IT ISN'T

There are different sorts of false teachers in the world of religion. Some admit to being religious teachers and utilize biblical or theological terms to present their systems. Sun Myung Moon, the self-acclaimed Messiah from Korea, and the recently deposed fifteen-year-old ''Perfect Master'' of a few years ago, Maharaj Ji, have identified themselves clearly as religious teachers, leaving no doubt in the minds of those who decide to become their followers that they are pursuing a religion, and not something else. Although reports of the mental conditioning in Moon's mission read like horror stories, and the average disciple of that Messiah hardly realizes the extent of his own brainwashing, at least there is a clear identification with religion in those movements, however shrewd and selfish the Messiahs.

But Maharishi is introducing a whole new ballgame into religion. Because the movement's publicity dishonestly represents TM to be non-religious, the average follower just doesn't realize that he is being drawn into Hinduism while seeking through meditation mental solace or whatever the local TM branch is offering at the moment. By the time the initiate becomes a knowledgeable meditator, it is a matter of faith with him to keep the secret. The dedicated TM teacher doesn't want to scare off new adherents by telling it like it is, so he makes some kind of bargain with his conscience to perpetuate the lie in the name of greater God-consciousness. The ex-teachers of TM we interviewed expressed their regret for having deceived people in order to get them into the fold. Describing TM as non-religious to the public, when they knew better, was one of the more difficult parts of being a TM teacher.

Somewhere along the line in any false religion the lie will be exposed. Most people have no fear of being candid about their religious beliefs but dedicated TM followers must carry the heavy secret with them that they are peddling Hinduism in a dishonestly non-religious wrapping. That the faculty of Maharishi International University are simply a group of liars is a strong statement; but we have given their exact words faithfully in this book so that the reader can make up his own mind, and be warned of the deceptions they practice.

When the true Messiah, Jesus, warned of false prophets, he was sounding a special warning for these closing days of world history. There have always been false religions and false preachers, but we are now seeing, in the age of public relations, a new kind of evangelist who is able to deceive many people into believing that he is not preaching a religion at all.

It works, and it is simply devastating!

THE TRANSLATED PUJA
This puja translation has been verified accurate by Maharishi and MIU officials
[Des Moines Register, Oct. 25, 1975;
Fairfield [Iowa] Ledger, Oct. 3, 1975]

INVOCATION

Whether pure or impure, whether purity or impurity is permeating everywhere, whoever opens himself to the expanded vision of unbounded awareness gains inner and outer purity.

INVOCATION

To LORD NARAYANA, to lotus-born BRAHMA the
Creator, to VASHISHTHA, to SHAKTI and his son
PARASHAR,
To VYASA, to SHUKADEVA, to the great GAUDA-
PADA, to GOVINDA, ruler among the yogis, to his
disciple, SHRI SHANKARACHARYA, to his disciples
PADMA PADA and HASTA MALAKA
And TROTAKACHARYA and VARTIKA KARA, to
others, to the tradition of our Masters, I bow down.

To the abode of the wisdom of the SMRITIS and PUR-
ANAS, to the abode of kindness, to the personified glory of
the LORD, to SHANKARA, emancipator of the world, I
bow down.

To SHANKARACHARYA the redeemer, hailed as
KRISHNA and BADARAYANA, to the commentator of
the BRAHMA SUTRAS, I bow down.
To the glory of the LORD I bow down again and again, at
whose door the whole galaxy of gods pray for perfection day
and night.

Adorned with immeasurable glory, preceptor of the whole
world, having bowed down to Him we gain fulfillment.

Skilled in dispelling the cloud of ignorance of the people, the
gentle emancipator, BRAHMANANDA SARASVATI,
the supreme teacher, full of brilliance, Him I bring to my
awareness.

Offering the invocation to the lotus feet of SHRI GURU
    DEV, I bow down.
Offering a seat to the lotus feet of SHRI GURU DEV,
    I bow down.

Offering an ablution to the lotus feet of SHRI GURU DEV,
I bow down.

Offering cloth to the lotus feet of SHRI GURU DEV,
I bow down.

Offering sandalpaste to the lotus feet of SHRI GURU DEV,
I bow down.

Offering full rice to the lotus feet of SHRI GURU DEV,
I bow down.

Offering a flower to the lotus feet of SHRI GURU DEV,
I bow down.

Offering incense to the lotus feet of SHRI GURU DEV,
I bow down.

Offering light to the lotus feet of SHRI GURU DEV,
I bow down.

Offering water to the lotus feet of SHRI GURU DEV,
I bow down.

Offering fruit to the lotus feet of SHRI GURU DEV,
I bow down.

Offering water to the lotus feet of SHRI GURU DEV,
I bow down.

Offering a betel leaf to the lotus feet of SHRI GURU DEV,
I bow down.

Offering a coconut to the lotus feet of SHRI GURU DEV,
I bow down.

OFFERING CAMPHOR LIGHT

White as camphor, kindness incarnate, the essence of
creation garlanded with BRAHMAN, ever dwelling in the
lotus of my heart, the creative impulse of cosmic life, to
That, in the form of GURU DEV, I bow down.

Offering light to the lotus feet of SHRI GURU DEV, I bow
down.

Offering water to the lotus feet of SHRI GURU DEV, I bow
down.

OFFERING A HANDFUL OF FLOWERS

GURU in the glory of BRAHMA, GURU in the glory of VISHNU, GURU in the glory of the great LORD SHIVA, GURU in the glory of the personified transcendental fullness of BRAHMAN, to Him, to SHRI GURU DEV adorned with glory, I bow down.

The Unbounded, like the endless canopy of the sky, the omnipresent in all creation, by whom the sign of That has been revealed in Him, to SHRI GURU DEV, I bow down.

GURU DEV SHRI BRAHMANANDA, bliss of the Absolute, transcendental joy, the Self-Sufficient, the embodiment of pure knowledge which is beyond and above the universe like the sky, the aim of Thou art That and other such expressions which unfold eternal truth, the One, the Eternal, the Pure, the Immoveable, the Witness of all intellects, whose status transcends thought, the Transcendent along with the three gunas, the true preceptor, to SHRI GURU DEV, I bow down.

The blinding darkness of ignorance has been removed by applying the balm of knowledge. The eye of knowledge has been opened by Him and therefore to Him, to SHRI GURU DEV, I bow down.

Offering a handful of flowers to the lotus feet of SHRI GURU DEV, I bow down.

FOOTNOTES: CHAPTER THREE

Introductory quotes: R.C. Zaehner, *Zen, Drugs, and Mysticism*, p. 72; *On The Bhagavad Gita*, p. 257; *Christian Century*, Dec. 10, 1975, p. 1125; A. Avalon, *The Serpent Power* (Dover, 1974), p. 204; *Aphorisms of Yoga*, p. 70; *Philosophy of Meditation*, p. 29.

1. Maharishi, *On the Bhagavad Gita*, pp. 291, 364.

2. *Ibid.*, pp. 440-1.

3. *Ibid.*, p. 441, cf. 172-4.

4. Maharishi, *Meditations*, p. 51.

5. Lecture at Berkeley TM center, July 19, 1975.

6. (Bantam, 1973), p. 8.

7. Maharishi, *Transcendental Meditation*, p. 272.

8. *Ibid.*, p. 268.

9. *Meditations*, p. 168.

10. Maharishi, *Gita*, pp. 262, 344; Maharishi, *Transcendental Meditation*, pp. 33, 194, 199, 263.

11. Robbins, Fisher, *op. cit.*, pp. 8, 119.

12. Denniston, McWilliams, p. 19.

13. Forem, *Transcendental Meditation*, p. 37.

14. *Ibid.*, p. 3.

15. Oct. 13, 1975.

16. Des Moines (Iowa) *Register*, Oct. 25, 1975.

17. Fairfield (Iowa) *Daily Register*, June 26, 1975.

18. Maharishi, *The Holy Tradition*, p. 5.

19. Wood, *Seven Schools of Yoga*, p. 88.

20. (Dickenson Pub. Co., 1971), pp. 110-12.

21. Forem, *op. cit.*, p. 238.

22. Maharishi, *Transcendental Meditation*, p. xii.

23. Jan. 1975, and Oct. 1974 respectively.

24. Maharishi, *Gita*, p. 365.

25. *Meditations*, p. 59.

26. *Ibid.*, p. 95.

27. Maharishi, *Gita*, p. 319.

28. *Ibid.*, pp. 317, 319.

29. *Ibid.*, p. 316.

30. *Ibid.*, p. 247.

31. *Ibid.*, p. 291.

32. *Meditations*, pp. 24, 57, 158, etc.

33. Maharishi, *Transcendental Meditation*, pp. 254-5.

"It is a kind of looking out on the world with the mind of God. In this state the subject is not aware of God; he is God."

—Una Kroll, M.D., describing
TM's "God-consciousness" state

"The state of transcendental consciousness is the state of Yoga, or Union, where the mind remains so completely united with the divine nature that it becomes It (*i.e.,* Brahman)."

—Maharishi

"I am the light of lights; I am the sun; I am the real, real, sun . . . In me the whole world moves and has its being . . . I existed before the world began . . . I permeate and pervade every atom . . . Oh, how beautiful I am . . . I am the whole universe; everything is in me . . . I am that."

—Swami Vishnudevananda, Yoga meditation

"It is meaningful to say that I cease to exist, becoming immersed in the ground of Being, in Brahman, in God, in 'Nothingness' . . . ."

—Aldous Huxley, describing
his experience under Mescalin

"In searching for a communicating word for discussions with my (TM) teacher, I chose *nothingness* to describe what was going on in my head during meditation. 'That's *fullness,*' she explained; 'that's Transcendental Meditation; that's Pure Consciousness. That's it."

—Terry Schaertel

"If we try to render this state into words we find ourselves descending into absurdity."

—Maharishi, describing
cosmic consciousness

"The question at stake is no common one; it is this: are we in our senses, or are we not?"

—Epictetus

CHAPTER FOUR

THE TM MYSTIQUE

Transcendental meditation works, as we have seen. It does have an effect, though the reasons for its effect are widely misunderstood. In this chapter, and the subsequent ones, we will examine the why and how of TM, and we will especially look into this matter of the price to be paid for personality alteration.

There are real dangers to TM and we wish to look at these very carefully. They are known, but never mentioned, by the TM promoters, who pass the program off as being much simpler and more innocuous than it really is.

TM's central objective is to alter the meditator's sense of personal identity and his outlook on the world around him. It is felt that life is full of suffering and that TM is designed to alleviate this suffering. It's certainly a noble enough goal, but the Master's way of achieving it is a matter of great concern, we feel. Suffering is allegedly alleviated through TM because a meditator comes to believe that he is God, and since God does not suffer, the meditator does not suffer.

Our problem, suggests Maharishi, is that we think we have a problem. When we come to the realization that we are divine all our problems are over. Maharishi says, ''The answer to every problem is that there is no problem. Let a man perceive this truth and then he is without problems.[1]''

Maharishi teaches that normal everyday activities are destructive unless one is permanently established in cosmic consciousness, the second level of TM. Everyday activities tyrannically keep us identified with the ''relative'' world and prevent us from achieving the ultimate reality—the realm of the Absolute, or pure Being (Brahman). As long as we wallow in this unreal world we continue to suffer and we fail to find the relief provided by realizing we are Brahman through TM.

Now Being—resting in Brahman—is opposed to action; hence we must still our action and still our minds. We must transcend all mental activity and arrive at the realm of Being. In this enviable state there is no awareness of any input from the world whatsoever—in fact, we are aware of nothing.

This ''zero awareness'' state is achieved several times during a typical meditation period and is described by meditators as ''blank awareness,'' or ''being awake inside with nothing going on,'' or ''not being asleep but being aware of nothing,'' etc. This state is to be highly desired, according to the guru, who calls it ''pure awareness.'' In this inactive state, which should be achieved daily, God and true Reality are encountered, according to Maharishi.

> Action is a veil which hides this essential nature of the Self.[2]

> The divine is completely separate from the field of activity. When this has been realized, the Self is experienced as independent of activity.[3]

> Happiness lies beyond the range of activity.[4]

Desire, in the state of ignorance [rather than in the informed state of cosmic consciousness], overshadows the pure nature of the Self, which is absolute bliss-consciousness [Brahman], and this keeps the life in bondage and suffering.[5]

Of course, this all assumes that one subscribes to the eastern concept that life is tough simply because we perceive it wrongly, and that our actions are always hopelessly off-base because of our misconceptions. Hence the guru's solution—utter inactivity, leading to God-consciousness—is supposed to save us a lot of heartache.

So Maharishi proposes that everyone practice temporary inactivity, mental and physical, each morning and evening. This doesn't sound like too bad an idea on the surface, but the guru informs us that through TM we will be cultivating a real personality change, little by little. Each time we achieve the initial state of relaxation that he calls transcendental consciousness, we are supposedly infusing into the mind a little more Being. We will actually be slowly altering the central nervous system, including the brain. The TM experience has a way of getting a strong hold on normal thinking processes and normal activities of the nerves and transforming them into Maharishi's state of Being.

The guru exults:

In the beginning of the practice [of TM], the Being [state] is very delicately impressed on the nature of the mind. But as the practice is continued, it becomes more and more deeply infused in the mind and eventually becomes so deep and significant and unshakeable that it is lived all the time through all the experiences of the wakeful, dreaming, and deep-sleep states. Then one lives eternal freedom in the life of relative experience.[6]

Through the regular practice of transcendental deep meditation the nature of the Being becomes steadfast in the very nature of the mind to such an extent that it can never be overshadowed by anything of relative order (normal life events). [7]

After some five years or so this state of temporary transcendental consciousness becomes transformed into the second level of TM, as we have seen, and the meditator enters cosmic consciousness, where the main difference is that his Being state is with him day and night. He doesn't have to ''go under'' to get there anymore—he's down there twenty-four hours per day!

At this level worldly activity is still engaged in, but the meditator now sees his Self as independent of all of his activities. His desires and actions in the world no longer have the detrimental effect of binding his personality to them. Worldly activities make no impression on the new true Self, so Maharishi says. The meditator and the world are separated.

TM's fourth level, or Unity consciousness as it is sometimes called, completely reunites the meditator and his environment, but under a new understanding. The meditator's Self is now divine and the world is divine, with no distinction left at all between the meditator and the world. All is now Brahman, on this final level, including the meditator and the world. All is One, all of the meditator's actions are really Brahman's actions, the meditator is at last one with God.[8] The Self is pervaded by God and God alone remains. Maharishi says of this state:

> Here is he who can speak for God . . . here is he who acts for God, here is the image of God on earth and the individual mind of man is the cosmic mind of God.[9] Then he and his God are one in himself.[10]

That long trip to Unity-consciousness is seldom spelled out just that way for novices, understandably. Such talk loses subscribers.

Maharishi seeks to assist each man in finding his true Self, so he says, since this is the only way men can live out their true natures. No problems, no suffering, no confusion can come to those totally pervaded by Brahman, and despite the arduous tour of states of consciousness involved, it is all worth it, according to the TM propaganda.

Cosmic consciousness—that state where the meditator achieves the separation of his Self from the rest of things—has been described by ex-TM teachers as somewhat similar to watching a movie. The action is up there all right, but the viewer can just observe it; he doesn't have to take part. The world outside is the movie on the screen, but the meditator can choose his role, or not act at all. Maharishi styles the feeling as the meditator being detached from himself so that he can watch himself act.[11] "We don't do anything and enjoy everything. Life should be lived from *that* level," Maharishi says.[12]

SO YOU WANT TO BE IN PICTURES

Watching one's life pass like a movie may not be the blissful trip Maharishi describes. It is rather the experience of drug abusers, from alcoholics to takers of uppers and downers and hard drugs, in their particualr "escape" from life's problems. It is also the euphoric sensation reported by those who are peacefully insane—life has gone off somewhere, along with all of its puzzles, and the former participant is now at rest.

But drinkers splash down eventually, and drug-abusers experience side effects. Usually the trip back into life—and life just won't go away for most of us—is a bumpy one. How much help Brahman really is, once it is reached, is unclear to anybody who hasn't been there, and we come back to taking TM on "faith."

Assuming that life is not real has moral implications as well. People side-stepping life with this philosophy sometimes get into a great deal of trouble. They *do* continue to function in life, which seems to have a way of closing in on them. The recognition of good and evil, fundamental to all religions, if not to all social transactions in general, becomes very fuzzy when life is looked upon as illusory. If, after all, one is out there riding on one's personal cloud, what does it matter if one happens to bump into a few bad situations if life isn't real anyway? Drug abusers tend to find trouble everywhere, commit crimes, and generally cut across the social fabric. Many ''heads''—drug addicts—undertake crimes for kicks, rather than just to finance their habits, and this seems to be related to a perversely maladjusted sense of right and wrong that comes with the drugs. Minds are impaired by the concept that life is not real.

The same consequences follow from the idea that Brahman (God) is everything. In the words of Charles Manson:

If God is One, what is bad? 13

It is important to realize that the beneficial effects claimed for TM are merely side effects not central to its true purpose. That one feels a lift after resting with the eyes closed is not very mysterious; that this lift is a step along the road to Maharishi' series of states of consciousness is the point. It seems that once the trip is begun, it becomes hard for the meditator to turn back. Having originally asked for a short journey to relaxation, he gets taken on a trip around the world, and then completely off of it! The vehicle in which he travels doesn't slow down and the driver refuses to tell the passenger where he is being taken. The passenger seems to finally forget who he is altogether and where he thought he was going, and Brahman steps in.

NO CHARGE FOR ALTERATIONS

As part of the TM meditating process you get your personality altered free of charge. You don't even know it's happening.

A reading of Maharishi's master plans in his books reveals immediately what TM is up to, [14] but even some TM teachers don't trouble to read them. Nor do most of the unwary initiates. But make no mistake about it, an altered personality—one which will finally conform to the Hindu view of the world—is the end result of TM. Maharishi, the God-realized yogi, states plainly:

> The seeker is exhorted to set himself on the path of transcendental meditation, gain Union of the mind with the divine Self in transcendental consciousness, realize that Self as separate from activity in cosmic consciousness, rise to God through devotion, and finally attain complete Union with Him. [15]

One becomes the happy prisoner of a God who takes care of everything, if all goes according to plan. In God and Unity consciousness, the guru says, ''Omnipresent silence [Brahman] works out everything for him [the meditator] and ''in this state the divine intelligence does everything for him . . . . It is as if everything were going by itself . . . . No diversity of life is able to detract from this state of supreme Unity. One who has reached It [Brahman] is the supporter of all and everything, for he is life eternal. [16] ''

Maharishi himself has reached this ultimate, labor-saving state of consciousness, of course, and can say of himself:

> By virtue of My Being, this mighty universe of huge and contrasting elements eternally and spontaneously exists, while I remain uninvolved. [17]

It's probably just as well. Many are not completely convinced that the world is a better place because Maharishi is in it, even if he says he is not the one responsible for running it. Some might say that the less involved the guru is the better off we all are, but that is for the meditators to discover. Maharishi is seldom described as purposefully evil, and he is often held to be an honest seeker diligently working toward his conception of a better life for everyone. A minority view holds that he is a good businessman, and *very* involved in *that.*

He seems to be an average phenomenon of the coming ''end times,'' quite in keeping with the warnings of Jesus.

ALL OR NOTHING

It should be very clear by now that the change effected in a personality by TM is intended to be permanent. Once started and practiced, the meditation tends to lead the meditator inexorably down the road to a permanent personality alteration. Maharishi says:

> When the mind, through the practice of transcendental meditation, rises to the state of cosmic consciousness, *absolute Being becomes permanently established in the nature of the mind,* and it attains the state of Brahman, the Universal Being. [18] (our emphasis.)

Psychiatrist Bloomfield, quoted above, agrees that:

> The repeated experience of unbounded energy, intelligence, and satisfaction [sat-chit-ananda, or Brahman] at the depth of the mind is so profoundly significant that *this experience supplants all previous identity formation.*[19] (our emphasis.)

When the guru gives you a permanent, you're his! The fact is, we arrive at our personal identities through our own personal storehouse of experiences. We collect pieces of life and put them into places in our minds, and there emerges a picture that makes sense to each of us, although the picture will vary from personality to personality. But a change in thinking patterns will often alter a personality, and repeated changes will permanently alter it.

TM, properly practiced, is repeated, doggedly, morning

and night, and it does dig deep into the mind. The mantra has the effect of dulling the mind to its normal perceptions so that the sensation of detachment sinks in deeply.

Maharishi values the repetition of the TM exercise, and its mixture with life's activities:

> The practice of meditation, and the activity that follows it—morning and evening meditation and activity during the day—develop a state in which the nature of mind *becomes transformed into the state of Being,* while the ability to act in all fields of practical life is fully maintained. [20] (our emphasis.)

One can only wonder at what Maharishi considers "all fields of practical life," in view of his summary dismissal of life as illusory. Perhaps this expression is one of those meant to seduce the casual observer of TM into thinking that it will have no profound effect on the way he does things. Actually, of course, we can deduce from Maharishi's other quotations above, that activity is greatly affected, curtailed in fact, by TM.

But the fact remains, "the nature of the mind becomes transformed," and furthermore, as Maharishi says, the meditator does not even realize the cause.

> When one meditates, one experiences increased energy and clarity of mind, but *does not experience* the actual process of the infusion of the Being (Brahman) into the nature of the mind. [21] (our emphasis.)

The effects are felt—the increased energy and clarity of mind—but the cause is concealed. Most beginners probably assume that TM is simply a beneficient way of handling the nerves. They fail to appreciate the doctrine behind the cure, of course.

WHICH WAY TO BRAHMAN?

So, how *does* it work? Why does TM produce results, and

finally persuade people that they have become One with Brahman?

Theologically we might answer that very simply. Brahman exists alright, but his real name isn't Brahman, and he's been deceiving people with new systems of knowledge since the Garden of Eden. He'll swap you anything at all for your undivided attention, but you'll have to pay the check.

The spiritual world is a peculiar place, the Bible attests, where unseen influences of all persuasions are at work. Mystics have generally supported a pantheistic theme: the Divine in everything, including themselves. Many mystical traditions hold this view of God, from psychic and mediumistic disciplines to UFO contacts, and to a lesser degree, biofeedback, LSD and schozophrenia.[22] It is an almost universal story—those with certain states of altered awareness experience powerful sensations of God in every direction, especially within themselves.

Actually, the mystics are right when they psychically perceive (or misperceive) the omnipresence of God, at least according to the Bible, which *does* define the nature of God (unlike the Hindu sacred books). But the mystic, usually without a modicum of Biblical knowledge to apply to spiritual situations, cannot see God as He is, distinct from His creation. Instead, the mystic misconceives God as pantheistic—"Being," "Brahman," or whatever other name—an all-pervasive "thing" in which one may have a greater and greater part until one unifies with It. The ultimate unspiritual step made by the mystic is to think that he himself is God, and this is where pantheism inevitably leads.

The Bible warns against occult-psychic involvement because of its skillful counterfeit of true revelation. Normally, cultic worship, like TM, leads the follower along a path superficially like the actual way to God as given in the Scriptures. The follower of Christ does meditate, does transcend worldly life to a degree and does finally unite with

God, but not in the TM way. This is through the grace of God, something He does for us rather than as a result of any special effort (like the repeating of a mantra) on the part of the seeker (Eph. 2:8-9). True salvation, as the Bible explains, is the free gift of God, not a prize won by man.

Unfortunately, cultic worship usually keeps the participant beyond the reach of true salvation. After all, if one has become God, one doesn't need to *come* to God. One does not need a Savior if one has succeeded in saving oneself. One is not separated from God by sin if one *is* God, and one always does the right thing if one is God. Repentance, if one is God, is out of the question, of course.

Recognizing the enemy who is responsible for such philosophies, we are forced to appreciate his brilliance in so successfully employing such deceptions. By promising men that they can become God, he has managed to keep men from God permanently. Maharishi and all of the other meditators seem to sincerely feel that they are approaching God (or have already become God) when, Biblically speaking, they are forfeiting all chance of that. More on that in a following chapter comparing TM and Christianity.

Medically speaking, the way to Brahman, or wherever the TM faithful actually go, may be related to physiological changes in the central nervous system. The central nervous system and the normal state of consciousness must be altered for the TM effect to take over. The normal human state of consciousness inhibits the state of transcendental consciousness, preventing us from slipping into such trances. This is a favor done by our nervous system. We cannot afford to keep tuning in and out on the world around us. But, according to Maharishi, "The practice of the mind in passing from one [TM state] to another gradually overcomes this physiological inhibition.[23]" Steady TM exercise tends to relax the natural aversion to "tuning out."

This function of TM doesn't seem like an entirely positive experience. The legendary stories about people on drug trips failing to perceive ordinary dangers, or losing common-sense inhibitions are legion. The all too true joke about the police who raided a drug party on an upper floor after finding a body in the street below is an illustration. Party-goer: "He said he wanted to fly over to the next building." Police: "Why didn't you stop him?" Party-goer: "Like, I thought he'd make it, man!"

Maharishi freely admits, "This state [Unity with Brahman] can only become permanent when the physical nervous system is sufficiently cultured [altered] to maintain it . . . [the] re-creation of the normal functioning of the entire system" [is necessary, and] "the very nature of the man" must be transformed in order for him to advance in TM.[24]

For those who enjoy their nervous sytem and bodily functions pretty much the way they functioned in the first place, the guru's proposals are a bit frightening:

> The re-orientation of the nervous system is essential in order to make permanent the state of transcendental consciousness, but it must be brought about by a mental process.[25]

So, the nervous system has to be permanently conditioned so that it can simultaneously support the normal consciousness, without which we simply cannot operate in the world, plus a permanent state of transcendental consciousness. This is the somewhat "schizophrenic" experience of cosmic consciousness.[26] To experience the transcendental state, the "activity of the brain has to cease" while conscious awareness of nothing but consciousness itself remains.[27] This is necessary because, "The process of thinking is opposed to the state of Being.[28]"

Obviously, if the model (our body) didn't come with the propensity to accommodate a dual state of consciousness, it seems hazardous to try to recondition it to do that. Theologically speaking, if we must radically change our minds and bodies to reach some god, he must be the wrong god. The One who created us made us perfectly in His own image, He said, and with the ability to reach Him easily.

Some physiological speculation has been done on TM as medical experimenters have become interested in the "change of consciousness" exercise. The central nervous system is one of the mysterious areas in medical research; we can't explain very exactly how *normal* consciousness operates, let alone altered consciousness, and the TM state of altered consciousness has caught the interest of doctors.

Dr. Anthony Campbell, M.D. theorizes that during TM "the activity of the thalamo-cortical systems (responsible for the content of consciousness) is reduced, while that of the reticulo-thalamic system (responsible for alertness) is maintained." He feels also that TM's cosmic consciousness "consists in a permanent modification in the amount or character of the activity of the reticulor-thalamic system.[29]" The permanent nature of the physiological alteration is the worrisome part, of course. Dr. Una Kroll, M.D., notes that TM can produce permanent physiological change in the individual.[30] Both doctors are TM supporters.

Many people approach TM as dabblers, looking for something new and interesting to do with themselves, and, as advertised, TM is merely a beneficial diversion. The customers might flock out of the store if they understood that TM plays for keeps.

There might be a traceable chemical effect with TM. Some researchers feel that the practice creates a new chemical substance in the body or gives a new usage to one already present, like the perception—altering serotonin. Maharishi agrees with this theory and calls the new substance "soma," noting it is mentioned by that name in the ancient Hindu Vedas. The guru says that soma is produced at the cosmic consciousness level and is an essential physiological component for further refinements in altered consciousness.[31]

Whether some really exists or not, it is true that the brain has experienced some reconditioning by the time it reaches the cosmic consciousness state of TM because this state is maintained, rather than coming and going like the lesser transcendental state. The change involved with cosmic consciousness is permanent. The brain tends to "remember" the state it goes into each day possibly via more and more familiar neural pathways triggered by the mantra. The introduction of the mantra as a triggering device is most effective, as researcher Dr. Bernard Glueck points out:

> It seems increasingly apparent from EEG (electro-encephalographic readings—brain waves) findings that the mantra is the significant element in the whole process, apparently able to markedly alter brain function within a matter of seconds.[32]

Apparently the steady practice of TM leads to increased alpha brain wave activity, which may become a permanent feature of the brain physiology of the meditator. Eventually the meditator's brain could steadily undertake this activity whether he is in meditation or not. If true, a minimum of 6 months of TM seems to be necessary for this change to occur.[33] The alpha waves are found below the normal conscious-thinking state (beta waves) and are associated with relaxation. The Silva Mind Control cult utilizes prolonged alpha states to induce spirit-contact and psychic powers, both possible with TM. Maharishi advocates that the entire population develop psychic powers via TM, and it is fairly well know among TM teachers that the higher TM states can lead one to experience contact with spirits—on *their* initiative (see appendix).

Theta rhythms are increased with TM, representing a deeper level still, where reincarnation "experiences" are reportedly found. These strange goings-back are reported by those practicing TM. One thinks of the different levels of hypnotic states in connection with these deepened levels of brain-wave activity. At the deepest level of these, far beneath what the dentist uses against pain, reincarnation experiences are also reported. Reincarnation is a standard feature of eastern religious mysticism and we would expect it to attend the TM experience (see appendix).

TM may condition new "pleasure centers" in the brain which provide the blissful feelings associated with the practice. In laboratory experiments with rats it has been found that the rat will sacrifice everything, even food and water, to press the lever that electronically stimulates the newly conditioned pleasure center in his brain. A rat will stand by this electronic bar and press it up to 8,000 times per hour, forgetting all else, to achieve the pleasure sensation. He will even "die trying." Likewise in TM, when one reaches the Unity with Brahman level there is supposed to be no greater sensation of perfect bliss and the meditator forsakes all else to pursue this. In our pleasure-centered society the idea of reaching such a state where tidal waves of joy overwhelm one may be the popularity feature of TM. Possibly a pleasure center is psychically conditioned in the human brain by the practice of this meditation. In any case, the devotees normally enjoy it. It is to be noted, however, that some who practice TM never realize this state of bliss.

WHAT PRICE BLISS?

Clearly, TM has an effect, and possibly a very pleasurable effect, but there is also a price that must be paid. The spiritual issue is this: while Hinduism's technique called TM can be comforting to some, it creates a *distorted* view of life, and actually takes the devotee away from God. It would be more reasonable to regard TM as Hinduism and then to compare its merits with Biblical Christianity on that basis. But as things are, TM continues its popular masquerade.

The scientific issue is not as clear yet, but there is good reason to suppose from the research that has been done that TM is in no objective way beneficial, and may indeed be harmful. The reconditioning of the brain so that it produces unusual patterns of waves is a scary and unexplored function of TM. The tuning out of the world, with its concomitant relaxation of normal caution, is known to be dangerous. The central nervous system, that fantastically complex network of bodily communication and sensation, should never be casually tampered with. The profound variations in normal human functioning required by TM, and cheered on by its guru, are undertaken only at the peril of the meditator.

The guru has obviously found a good thing here in the west. In societies already conditioned to think great pleasure is just around the corner, he comes laden with promises of unmitigated bliss.

And like rats pressing a pleasure bar, we follow by the millions!

FOOTNOTES : CHAPTER FOUR

Introductory quotations : *The Healing Potential of Transcendental Meditation* (John Knox, 1975), p. 44; *On the Bhagavad Gita*, p. 183; *The Complete Illustrated Book of Yoga*, p. 351; Zaehner, *Zen, Drugs and Mysticism*, p. 105; *Impact*, Nov. 1972; Anthony Campbell, *The Seven States of Consciousness*, p. 69; *The Harvard Classics*, LXXIV, p. 144.

1. Maharishi, *On the Bhagavad Gita*, p. 66.

2. *Ibid.*, p. 338.

3. *Ibid.*, p. 342.

4. *Ibid.*, p. 350.

5. *Ibid.*, p. 237.

6. Maharishi, *Transcendental Meditation*, p. 56.

7. *Ibid.*

8. Maharishi, *Transcendental Meditation*, pp. 248-9, 268; Maharishi, *Gita*, pp. 172-3, 209-11, 225-6, 273, 292-3, 448; Kroll, *op. cit.*, p. 46.

9. *Ibid.*

10. Maharishi, *Gita*, p. 448, quoting ch. 4:48.

11. *Ibid.*, p. 223.

12. Maharishi, "The Seven States of Consciousness," a recorded talk (last of two statements).

13. *Rolling Stone*, June 25, 1970.

14. Maharishi, *Transcendental Meditation*, pp. 56, 122, 233, 278-9; Maharishi, *Gita*, pp. 142, 184, 211, 251, 172-3, 209-11, 225-6, 271-3, 276, 288, 344, 392-8, 448, 467, 412-17, 381-468; Maharishi, "The Seven States . . ." and Campbell, *The Seven States of Consciousness* (Perennial, 1974) for TM levels and documentation.

15. Maharishi, *Gita*, p. 381.

16. *Ibid.*, pp. 341, 392-3, 448-9.

17. *Ibid.*, pp. 414, 341, cf. 449 and Maharishi, *Love and God* (MIU Press, 1973), pp. 45, 52.

18. Maharishi, *Gita*, p. 360.

19. *TM: Overcoming Stress and Discovering Inner Energy*, p. 188.

20. Maharishi, *Gita*, p. 344.

21. Maharishi, *Transcendental Meditation*, p. 55.

22. Jodi Lawrence, *Alpha Brain Waves* (Avon, 1972), pp. 173, 220; White, ed., *The Highest State of Consciousness* (Anchor, 1972), pp. 187, 258-72, 279-91, 304-8, 313, 459; R.C. Zaehner, *Zen, Drugs and Mysticism* (Vintage, 1974), pp. 66-79, 85, 105, 109; *Chandogya Ypanishad:* 7.25.1; Maharishi, *Gita*, p. 412; UFO contacts have stated: "God is the universe;" Lawrence LeShan, *How to Meditate* (Bantam, 1975), p. 126; Campbell, *op. cit.*, p. 111 (epilepsy).

23. Maharishi, *Gita*, p. 314; Maharishi, *Transcendental Meditation*, p. 286. The inhibition is actually against the simultaneous function of normal and transcendental consciousness.

24. Maharishi, *Gita*, pp. 416-7.

25. *Ibid.*, p. 431.

26. *Ibid.*, p. 226.

27. Maharishi, *Transcendental*, p. 287.

28. *Ibid.*, p. 102.

29. Campbell, *op. cit.*, p. 72.

30. Kroll, *op. cit.*, p. 150.

31. Bloomfield, *op. cit.*, pp. 205-6; Zaehner, *op. cit.*, p. 81.

32. *Ibid.*, p. 102.

33. Lawrence, *op. cit.*, p. 174; Naranjo and Ornstein, *op. cit.*, p. 216.

34. Maharishi, *Transcendental Meditation*, pp. 98-99, cf. *Meditations*, pp. 17-18; Maharishi, *Gita*, p. 201 (The powers are gods—pp. 197-99).

"The TM program has no adverse side effects and can promote what pills cannot—natural psychological growth."

—Harold Bloomfield,
meditator and psychiatrist

"That the dangers of meditation *are* considerable among the immature appear to be overlooked by these (TM) enthusiasts who regard meditation as a universal panacea."

Una Kroll, M.D.

"It's so heavenly to be out of myself—when I'm everything, you know, and everything else is me."

—Medium Mrs. Willet,
describing her trance state

"In the state of God-consciousness, the mind is completely taken over by the unity of life."

—Maharishi

"There are risks in cultivating altered states of consciousness. One of these risks . . . may be a permanent alienation from ordinary human attachments."

—Elsa First, Child Psychotherapist

"As a person enters or is in an ASC (altered state of consciousness), he often experiences fear of losing his grip on reality and losing his self-control."

—Arnold M. Ludwig

''If one slaps a child in anger, then one has slapped or beaten the whole universe and produced an atmosphere of crying and hatred, suffering and discord—not only in the child but all around him and in the universe.''

—Maharishi

CHAPTER FIVE

A BAD TRIP

There is concern over whether some people can go absolutely nuts practicing TM.

We discussed briefly some of the psychological variables associated with meditation of this sort in the preceding chapter. In this section we want to dig deeper into the mental ramifications of the TM experience. The full consequences are not very well understood yet, but there are some dramatic indications that TM is not good for everybody, to say the least.

We should say, to begin with, that most meditators experience pleasurable sensations and personally satisfying results from TM. But, as we will show in this chapter, there exists in TM a mechanism which can foster serious psychopathology.

Let us share the following letter, supplied to us by a Berkeley researcher. It seems to be an advertisement for a specific kind of psychotherapy exclusively attuned to the problems of meditators, if we interpret it correctly. Here it is verbatim, including the title.

SHAMANISTIC HEALING

Brothers and sisters,

"Schizophrenia" is not an illness. It's a psychological space we can be in, another reality.

In our culture the "schizophrenic" experience frightens most folks and there are no shamans around to validate you and help you develop your abilities. You feel isolated and your family and friends try to convince you that you're sick and need help.

If you'd been born into a shamanistic culture, then undergone the "schizophrenic" experience, folks would have realized you were being selected as a shaman healer.

I've been a "schizophrenic." Now I'm a shaman healer. If we agree to work together I can help you be one too.

(Signature, followed by the designation "Howling Wolf," Ph.D., clinical psychology, with address and phone number.)

Doubtless many people would think that Howling Wolf is still a schizophrenic, whatever else he may have become through occultism; but he is apparently making some effort to help those who have also been diagnosed as schizophrenic to find their rightful place in "another reality." Schizophrenia is a serious psychological disorder. Characterized by a psychosis where the patient has lost touch with reality, it is usually treated by confinement with intensive psychotherapy and tranquilizing drugs, and the rate of cure is discouraging.

Dr. Wolf (his signature showed a common American name but his tribal-sounding designation is probably more expressive of his healing work) believes that what has been termed a mental illness by our western culture is actually an advantageous circumstance in eastern thinking. It supposedly provides a gift of healing, but subjects the gifted one to great misunderstanding from family and friends, not to mention psychiatrists.

The question is, would Howling Wolf have any patients at all if they didn't make themselves sick to begin with? That is, if deliberately altering states of consciousness, such as through drug abuse and TM, were discontinued, would this strange healer find himself short of clients? Did the new medicine bring on the new illness?

There is a temptation to think that Howling Wolf has something here and we have been shamefully accusing some very wise but very different-seeming people of mental illness. After all, scizophrenia is merely a word picked by psychotherapists to characterize a state of behavior they find abnormal. In these days of asylum confinement for dissidents in Russia, ought we not be more careful in calling people sick? Will we someday start calling Christians mentally ill because of their beliefs? Oughtn't we just live and let live when it comes to religions and mental exercises?

Possibly so, if the religions and practices involved clearly indicated to their devotees where they may be heading. But the characteristics of many of the new disciplines resemble out and out swindles because of the false advertising. Probably not one person in a hundred who undertakes TM knows that he is courting a new mental state of affairs, a new level of consciousness, to be followed by still more new levels, and a totally new outlook on what he thinks of as reality. The deceptive nature of the sales pitch is certainly one cause for serious concern.

In the drug trade the pusher rarely explains to the new customer that he will eventually be so totally hooked that he will have to invest huge sums of money in his habit, and possibly be even obliged to commit crimes to support it. That's not the way to get customers, obviously. With TM one has that same feeling about the seller taking unfair advantage of the buyer. If a well-informed consumer of TM could say at the outset, "Yes, I understand they're going to say I'm crazy later on; and yes, it is clear to me that I will develop a pantheistic view of the universe and a whole new concept of reality," most people would probably say, "Let him go ahead if he likes." But the idea of utterly *uninformed* people, especially youth, being led down some primrose path to what this culture, at least, thinks of as mental illness is too much for most westerners to stomach. Maybe Maharishi has something—but let him say plainly what he is offering for sale.

THE TM MENTALITY

We will discuss TM in this chapter in its relation to unique mental states: hypnosis, mysticism, insanity and suicide. We won't be soft-pedaling the fact that this meditation practice sometimes leads to utter disaster, though it is admittedly sometimes harmless. We will thoroughly document our discussion with the research that has been done on TM in the psychological areas.

There is sufficient evidence to indicate that TM is potentially very hazardous. The hazards do not apply to everyone, nor necessarily even to a majority, but they are unpredictable in individual cases because of the abnormal nature of the TM mental states. It should be said that those who drop out of the program soon enough, usually before seven months, and have had no negative mental experiences until then with TM, probably will remain unaffected. However, a certain varying percentage of those who pursue this program are letting themselves in for problems perhaps solvable only in the healing sphere of Dr. Howling Wolf. The problems will typically not be attributed to TM, because of its preconceived beneficial nature, compounding the difficulty.

To begin with, TM claims for itself a unique psychological state of mind with totally unique results. Supposedly no one could achieve the same effect with any other mental process but TM, which is Maharishi's exclusive technique developed during his two-year cave-sit. Although its roots lie deep in the ancient mystical traditions of India, TM is patented today for today's problems. It is in a class by itself, according to its publicity.

We differ with these claims right from the start. TM is actually an old, old story. Repetitious incantations to break down mental awareness have been in use for millennia. It is really not even exclusive to the Hindus. Mystical forms of consciousness are induced similarly in western hypnosis, in seances, in rock music, through various drugs, and in any number of cultic religions.

The common element in all withdrawal from the real world is the restriction of the mind to one single, unchanging process, whether the repetition of pre-designed formulae or a mantra. Nor does the psychic state reached by such practices vary much. Those who chant, engage in repetitious ritual, or simply dull the mind with repeated nonsense sounds, all seem to end up at the same place. We all have the same nervous system, after all. It shouldn't be surprising, then, that with similar inputs we all seem to take similar trips. We end up at basically the same places mentally, whether we travel by TM, drugs, hypnosis, or any other of a number of mental vehicles. TM is not special at all in this sense.

The brain wave research that has seemed to indicate that TM produces different wave patterns than sleep, wakefulness, hypnosis, etc., does not really prove any beneficial uniqueness for TM either. The brain is not the mind, and physiological measurements do not necessarily define mental experiences. LSD research, as well as TM research, shows that there is really little correlation between the subject's report of what he has experienced and the EEG reading of what his brain is doing. [1] A patient can be having an actual focal seizure, even be in a coma, and the EEG may show no abnormality.[2] One TMer produced theta waves that drove the recording pen right off the graph paper, but he subsequently rated his experience as only "fair.[3]" Brain wave activity with TM, as we said in the last chapter, is cause for concern but in no way makes TM a unique mental experience.

HIP HYPNOSIS

TM enthusiasts don't like comparisons between their program and ordinary hypnosis, but some research has shown that Maharishi's meditation system may be much like deep hypnosis. If the TMers are just hypnotizing themselves, all their magic loses its zing, of course. Rather commonplace in the west, both in medicine and entertainment, hypnosis usually costs less than $125 and a change of religion.

Maharishi admits that self-hypnosis is a valid way to Hinduism's God-realization,[4] opening up the suspicion that all one has to do to reach the guru's god is to blank himself out. He is careful, of course, not to equate TM with hypnosis, and so are his PR people. Convincing research, however, has shown a definitive correlation. A careful comparison of several reputable definitions of the states of hypnosis and auto-hypnosis with the TM state shows at least ten points in common.[5]

The TM promoters say that their program is vastly different from hypnosis physiologically[6] (e.g., oxygen consumption is typically different), but the long list of similarities is very persuasive nevertheless. And we are really comparing *mental* states, which is a different matter than physiological phenomena. Mentally, TM and auto-hypnosis look very much alike indeed, and TM may be just an up-to-date, fashionable form of hypnosis—a hip hypnosis.

Six reputable authorities have defined TM as simply a form of auto-hypnosis.[7] Hypnotism and yoga in general, which TM actually is, are said to be quite closely related.[8] Dr. Charles T. Tart of the University of California at Davis conducted research on exceptionally deep hypnosis, utilizing 13 different variables with which a hypnotized subject reported his "depth" of hypnosis. Dr. Tart took the patient to a depth level 130, on a scale where deep hypnosis was 30-40 and profound hypnosis was 50. In 11 of the 13 variables the reported designations by the subject were markedly similar to those characterizing the advanced TM states.[9] Dr. Tart noted that hypnosis in general smacked of the ability to exercise "magical power over others," and that the very profound level of hypnosis was essentially the same as reaching the Hindu state of "the Void."

TM—A BAD TRIP?

Mysticism and TM are deeply associated, though the TM public relations line is that the practice is perfectly "natural." Actually, the TM experience is more closely related to the types of mystical states achieved through psychedelic drugs. Again, the results bear a more than coincidental similarity.

Walter Pahnke, former Director of Clinical Sciences Research at Maryland State Psychiatric Research Center and associated with the John Hopkins University Medical School developed a nine-category typology of the mystical state (defined as experiences of unity, transcendance of space and time, behavior and attitude changes, and so forth). Pahnke utilized the research, in turn, of such scholars as William James and W.T. Stace, in his own study of the psychedelic experience. All of the nine categories are typical of the advanced TM experience, a thorough-going mystical state.

Pahnke found the mystical state and the drug state very closely related:

Those subjects who received psilocybin (related to LSD and mescalin) experienced phenomena that were apparently indistinguishable from, if not identical with, certain categories defined by the typology of mystical consciousness.[10]

It may serve to shed some light on the TM experience if it is understood as the mystical experience it really becomes with practice. That the same experience seems achievable either through drugs or by the Hindu pursuit of Brahman, gives TM a rather adverse connotation. The guru is the first to laud the highest mystical experiences in TM, equating them with Oneness with God (the "Unity" experience). But if like results come from damaging the mind with hard drugs, Maharishi's patented path to bliss is very suspect. TM then becomes just another bad trip, from which one may be permanently damaged.

Pahnke, Stace, Jordan and any number of other researchers have noted the close relationship between LSD states and mysticism.[11] Pahnke says:

Only in mystical consciousness, and some psychotic reactions, is the subject-object dichotomy transcended and the empirical ego extinguished.[12]

Or, in simpler terms, only during mystical experiences and some types of insanity does the human mind lose its grasp on the difference between the meditator himself and his surroundings. The expression "empirical ego extinguished" compares rather exactly with Maharishi's "the individual ceases to exist—he becomes pure existence.[13]" The mystical experience, like TM's "Unity," mixes up the medium with the messenger, and the individual becomes "at one" with the universe. Describing this feeling, TM enthusiasts make it sound like a great achievement—"I and the whole universe are one divine entity!"—but in the sober terms of Dr. Pahnke it is found in "some psychotic reactions.'' Research indicates that insane people experience this same peculiar extreme of consciousness and express it in terms almost identical to those used to describe the TM state of unity consciousness. Moreover, certain functions of TM practice, particularly ''unstressing'' and the personal divinity experience, are also found in mediumistic and LSD states.[14]

It seems, by Maharishi's own encouraging philosophy, that the mystical experience is greatly to be desired. Indeed, seasoned TMers go after it with a vengeance (a ''quiet'' vengeance) every day. But to find out that this hard-won mental state is intimately related to the ''highs'' gotten by drug abusers and even by some of the insane, is to make one wonder if it's all worth it.

LSD is more expensive than TM in many ways, though seemingly more efficient for those who wish to take a long trip. The destination of both trips seems to be the same, which raises an interesting question: would anyone want to go there in the first place?

With LSD, publicity and penalties have finally gotten through to the drug abusers and its popularity has been declining. Even the most far-out rebel can see the clear difference between a revolution for a cause and simply damaging his mind and body. Committed radicals won't touch the stuff anymore.

But TM is more sinister. There are no penalties for it; and its publicity, managed ably by the guru and his company of zealots, makes it sound like the Mr. Clean of mystical experiences. How could anybody get into any difficulty simply relaxing twice a day?

HOWLING WOLF LIVES

Howling Wolf, our clinical psychologist whose letter we quoted at the beginning of the chapter, will never run out of clients. There are more than a few schizophrenic TMers around, and for good reason. The program certainly doesn't cause everybody who undertakes it to lose his mind, as we explained above; but it is safe to say that the possibility is there for anyone indulging in this activity. Dr. Wolf has his work cut out for him.

There is nothing "natural" about TM despite all the claims to the contrary. Obviously, since the meditator must adopt a new and very special regimen which he has never encountered before, the activity is not one that comes naturally. The idea of repeating and repeating a nonsense sound in the mind is in no way natural, and not at all the way the mind ordinarily works. The mental state induced by this practice is not by any means a natural one. On the contrary, as we have seen, it is most closely associated with those mental states experienced by people who have suffered mental derangement of some kind.

Of course "natural" is a very good PR word nowadays. We have natural cereals, natural laxatives, natural cosmetics and a margarine so "natural" that it leads one to total disaster because "It's not nice to fool Mother Nature." Maharishi bends over backwards to connect TM and natural mental processes:

> Each mind has a natural inclination, a natural instinct, a natural faculty to go to a field of greater happiness . . . . This is the natural tendency of the mind.[15]

Few would quibble with that very natural statement by the guru, but his relating it to TM causes us to wonder. Naturally the statement is meant to give the good name of "nature's way" to his program.

In fact, TM practice puts the mind into a most uncomfortable and unnatural state of paradox. We can understand Howling Wolf's confusion when Maharishi calls the TM mental state "the void of abstract fullness" and "activity and no activity.[16] " Paradoxes which are supposed to be non-paradoxes (schizophrenia is normal; reality is not reality) confound the mind and make it dysfunctional.

THE SANITARY MIND

Maybe as Maharishi asserts, we have all been misperceiving the world. Maybe we are all deluded by illusions we think are real. All that granted, we still put our minds to a cruel test when we try to recondition them to see things so differently. First of all, Maharishi may be wrong. Secondly, few minds can stand that kind of reorientation. And finally, who's to say that our new perceptions will really bring the bliss that the guru promises? In spite of all the TM being practiced, the Age of Enlightenment still seems as far away as ever.

When an outside interpreter is needed to assuage the pain of going to a new TM state of consciousness we get suspicious. Learning in the western style—advancing in mathematics, say—does take energy and the learner feels some strain. But he hardly needs a healer to assure him that he is not going mad. Howling Wolf's practice, we notice, is confined to those who have lost their grip, or at least those whose family and friends think they have lost their grip. Dr. Wolf is out to soothe away fears of schizophrenia. It would seem better not to court the possibility of schizophrenia in the first place.

There seem to be enough paradoxes in what we perceive of the real world to begin with. We really don't need new ones. The guru's system gets a lot of mileage out of the mere fascination with new and different philosophies; but the fun goes out of TM, to say the least, when the mind, tuned to the real world with all of its real paradoxes, begins to balk at the strange new mysticism. While ''socially integrated'' schizophrenia is thought of as a state of higher consciousness in Hinduism, it has been established, by psychological testing against unquestionable norms, as insanity in the west. The "bad trip" aspect of TM is that "crazy equals sane." And not only "sane," but enviably advanced and close to God.

The career of Shaman-initiated Meher Baba, reported in *The God Man,* details the extremes of mental illness which may be suffered by the Hindu in pursuit of God. Baba endured the classic Shaman initiation, which involves periods of temporary insanity (defined as progress toward the higher states), and went on to minister to the insane in Indian society. He spent thirteen years among the "masts" of India, the insane, whom he considered spiritually advanced even though they could not function in society.[17] C.B. Purdom describes how they became insane: "(1) Those whose minds become unbalanced through unceasing dwelling upon thoughts about God so that they neglect all normal human requirements. (2) Those whose minds become unbalanced by sudden contact with a highly advanced spirit being. (3) Those who seek spiritual experience and meet a crisis from which they do not recover. What characterizes all is concentration upon the love of God.[18]"

Baba himself suffered severe insanity on his path to Hindu God-realization. He repeatedly would bang his head against walls and stones for months on end during lengthy trance states, and would be obliged to wrap his head in cloth to hide his wounds from his family. He went through aimless wanderings, severe disassociation and a long stream of schizophrenic symptoms in his pilgrimage.[19]

Whether Baba ever found God is not really very clear, nor is the particular god he was looking for. Manifestly clear, however, is the fact that Baba went on a very bad trip. If *that* is natural behavior, then we in the west indeed have a lot to learn; but the bruising of one's own head suggests that the course of study is better omitted.

MIND GAMES

The main difference between the out-and-out western schizophrenic, institutionalized and under care, and the mystic, loose in society but having the same experiences, lies in their differing ability to integrate their experience successfully into daily living. This in turn may depend upon how their mental state has been defined for them.[20] The mystic thinks of his state as bringing him closer to God, and he thus values it highly and will not be dissuaded from pursuing it still further. The mental patient has accepted that he needs help (or someone has certified this on his behalf), and he seeks a return to normality. Dr. Wolf, our Berkeley Shaman, wishes to redefine for schizophrenics their condition so that they will realize their good fortune. It takes a lot of patience with the Hindu view of things to accept his philosophy.

TM, to give it its due, is more careful with its seekers than other forms of Hinduism, cautiously nurturing its devotees from state to state of consciousness. The initiate into TM is supposed to gradually learn to accept the oncoming new states and integrate them into his personality without panic. The mystic states are consistently defined for the meditator as "higher consciousness" and he retains some grip on his personality, crediting himself for advancement. He is taught to control the new states step by step.

But obviously, this is a dangerous game. The steady pushing of the mind out to its sanity limits to achieve some new perception may be really asking for it. Who can say when a supposedly carefully controlled minor psychotic symptom might explode into a full-blown, incapacitating psychosis? Suppose one loses one's mind while controlling it? Can it be gotten back? Is there an antidote for the very bad TM trip? Can Maharishi get you back home after you've traveled so far? Or will you have to consult Howling Wolf, Ph.D.?

TM is defined as a higher form of mysticism which is socially integrated. The TMer can live in society and still have his mystical thing. The lower forms of mysticism, as they are defined, include the lost ones like India's masts and like the proverbial western schizophrenic who has become Napoleon in his own mind. But there is a suspicion that this distinction between the levels is not so clear.[21] William James noted that in both the higher and lower forms of mysticism the same "voices" were heard, "visions" came, and the "controlling by extraneous powers" was experienced.[22] Whether the mysticism is socially integrated or not, the symptoms seem to be the same, and this suggests that TM is no safer than the standard Hindu bad trips. In Hinduism, there even exists an "enlightenment" of pure evil.[23]

To Maharishi, the individual outside the level of cosmic consciousness is the true unfortunate. Abnormality, to the guru, involves going on with our hopeless misconceptions about the world, and failing to achieve his cosmic consciousness. But, in truth, we who continue to operate on our elementary level of consciousness don't seem to encounter the schizophrenic experiences that some TMers do. We bumble along, functional and socially integrated, even finding God by time-honored Biblical means, and we continue to think that mysterious voices and visions and external control are crazy.

It's enough to drive a guru sane!

SCHIZOPHRENIC SEMANTICS

Several researchers and former TM enthusiasts are convinced that TM can lead directly to impaired mental functioning and can be the very definition of a bad trip. Former TM teacher Gregg Randolph had the distressing experience of helping a nearly incapacitated and very frightened fellow-meditator through the cosmic consciousness transition:

At one time he was very concerned as to whether or not this was a state of schizophrenia. This worried him. We spent three hours one day trying to draw upon the resources that Maharishi drove into our minds in those teacher training courses . . . . The problem I had to help him with was that he had to start believing that it wasn't schizophrenia. This is the supreme state of knowledge . . . . He's just got to have faith that he's going to grow into this . . . and be able to handle it. Faith becomes a very important thing.[24]

Maharishi counsels, "In the absence of a proper interpretation of this expression of non-attachment, one might become bewildered, and this great blessing of life might become a liability.[25]"

Integrating the cosmic consciousness experience into an ongoing lifestyle is the crux of the problem. Psychiatrist Arthur Janov, author of *The Primal Scream*, tells of a senior Vedanta Monk who practiced TM for some 12 years. "The final result of all this bliss was a complete breakdown and the need for therapy." Dr. Janov feels that TM leads to "a state of total unreality, a socially institutionalized psychosis, as it were.[26]"

Among borderline psychotics TM "can bring on full-blown psychosis," says John White,[27] and it is generally conceded that one should be "in shape" for strenuous mental exercises, or one courts real trouble. TM requires quite a mental adjustment and seems to be just too much for people unprepared for such changes. Unfortunately it is usually tired, frustrated, worn-out people who seek just such panaceas as TM.

John Parks, former manager of The Beach Boys, was initiated into TM by Maharishi personally. He was thus in a position to know the inside story. He had the opportunity of seeing that TM can be exhausting and dangerous. Apparently Maharishi had not appreciated at that early date,

1969, that some Americans were just not ready for his system. Parks reports concerning a 1969 teacher training course:

> Maharishi had not put a time limit on meditating and quite a few people ended up in the mental hospital. Some are still there.[28]

Since that time, TM has become more carefully controlled, with suggested time limits and so forth, but it appears that the guru himself originally failed to understand the potency and hazardous nature of his trip to bliss. Possibly the Indian Hindus are able to follow a stricter regimen, with their long suffering mentality and general respect for marathon meditating, but Maharishi found, by trial and error with unsuspecting experimental subjects, that he had to take it easier over here. Unfortunately some of those original meditators are still hospitalized six years later. Maharishi's currently available book, *Transcendental Meditation,* still advocates "long hours of deep meditation."[29]

The TM propensity for causing mental illness seems built into the meditating procedure. Dr. Mike Miller of the Neuropsychiatric Institute at UCLA told co-author John Weldon:

> TM directs the individual to focus on the repetition of a mantra with the ultimate goal of Unity consciousness. Another way of stating this ultimate goal of TM is to become one with absurdity. TM carried to its logical conclusion is insanity.[30]

Maharishi describes the TM state as one "where the mind has renounced everything and is left alone by itself." He says of cosmic consciousness, "If we try to render this state into words we find ourselves descending into absurdity.[31]"

Paul Twitchell, an advanced occultist and deceased leader of the admittedly dangerous system of Eckankar ("the ancient science of soul travel''), is in a position to know what is dangerous in this nether area of mental experimentation. He warns, ''Many of these people who practice transcendental meditation are only going to increase their own neuroses. Schizophrenia is a very great danger in this kind of Indian meditation.[32]''

THE HARD WAY OUT

There are cases of TM suicides.

Chuck Ashman of ''The Ashman File,'' KTTV, Los Angeles, discovered a few instances in his TM inquiry, although he was not particularly looking for them.[33] He was really investigating the financial side of TM for his television talk show.

One of the most damaging statements to the TM program ever to come out is that of former TM instructor Kathy Filler, whose total disillusionment with the guru's program is easy to understand:

> But once we became teachers and started teaching people, I found out why the suicide rate for Transcendental Meditation teachers is way over the national average. The ones that don't kill themselves either get really weird or eventually drop back into drugs, or just fall apart—become crazy or recluses (so) that they just can't function. It's just a really sad thing. This is not something that I'm just making up. This is something that's been mentioned by Charlie Lutes (president of SRM) in the teacher's meditation courses. The last one attended was in 1972, Thanksgiving, in Asbury Park, New Jersey, and Charlie Lutes was there. People were asking about the suicide rate—teachers were asking why so many were killing themselves. He said, ''Well, in future incarnations, Maharishi will appear to them himself, or Guru Dev, and give them their mantra . . . [34]''

The astounding part is Lutes' casual treatment of the hard way out. People were actually taking their own lives in desperation—experienced teachers of TM—and he had no excuses or reasons, but only good wishes for some future incarnation!

Lutes' attitude perhaps serves to show the dogmatic devotion to the program inspired in the disciples by Maharishi. Even death—self-inflicted—is no cause for alarm, but holds good promise for the ''future!''

Una Kroll, M.D., writing in the London Times the following June mentioned the possibilities of TM-induced suicide and even murder among the other considerable dangers of the program. [35]

Perhaps we are going overboard, you may be thinking. There are some suicides associated with the stock market, with love affairs. A lot of people are mentally ill and that's all there is to that. Some of them get involved in TM and give it a bad name, perhaps.

THE SINISTER MECHANISMS

Actually, informed inquiry into the mechanism of the TM practice shows good reason why TM-related suicide exceeds the national average and why even murder becomes a possibility with TM. There are cogent and well-understood traps in the very process of the program that lead in terribly negative psychological directions.

Even Maharishi admits that TM if misunderstood can lead to bewilderment, confusion, fear, a blocking of emotional flow and a stressful and upset nervous system. [36] TM is powerful stuff. It actually amounts to placing the meditator in an acute state of sensory deprivation, where ordinary information from the environment does not come in. This is a model of insanity for many psychologists. [37] We need the continual reports by our senses on the world around us to function appropriately. But Maharishi says, ''Only when sensory perception has come to an end can the transcendental field of the Being be reached.[38]"

TM is a monotonous technique that produces alpha and theta waves in the brain activity—conditions associated with the production of spontaneous visualizations, or imagery ("visions").[39] Occultist J.H. Brennan warns that to mix yoga postures and visualizations without knowing exactly what one is doing "is asking for psychosis.[40]" Advanced TM does involve the yoga postures and yoga breathing coupled with meditation. The technique is known as "rounding," and psychiatrists warn of its dangers.[41] Yoga authority Ernest Wood terms dangerous the type of breathing exercise utilized in rounding.[42]

THE STRESS FACTOR

The TM technique called "unstressing," or what the guru refers to as normalizing the nervous system, can allow unconscious and repressed material to flood the normal consciousness.[43] This is a hazardous condition, entered into normally only under the supervision of a psychotherapist, and at great peril due to the sensory-deprivation situation. Anxiety lasting for many hours has resulted from "unstressing," as well as attacks of acute anxiety which mimic "losing the mind.[44]" In this painful condition an already mentally weakened individual reasonably can contemplate ending it all. Conversely he can grow very angry and hostile. He may want to kill—himself, or someone else—if his unrepressed hostility seems to warrant it.[45]

Dr. Goleman of Harvard, quoted above, notes that the unstressing technique can occur in "disturbing forms," and that "psychiatric clinics are beginning to get new patients who have been meditating on their own all day for many days . . . . The dynamics of this influx are parallel to the continuing wave of 'bad trips' due to drugs.[46]"

William Johnson, author of *Silent Music, The Science of Meditation*, notes that two dangers confront seekers of "higher consciousness"—withdrawal from the world, and too rapid or premature an entry into the higher states of consciousness—both possible in TM. He says that when either of these dangers occurs, "a person may find himself unable to control and integrate the images and the knowledge that suddenly flood his psyche." Johnson urges those curious about meditation to consult with a doctor before even beginning the procedure, and to keep in touch with that doctor for later distinguishing between "enlightenment" and downright mental illness. [47]

It's not so far-fetched. We indicated previously that the distinction between the guru's latter states of bliss and utter madness were blurred, and the meditators could be very frightened of what happens as they enter a new state. The following description of a Hindu devotee arriving at "enlightenment" is distressing:

> I thought I was dying. The whole body was, as it were, on fire, mind was being broken to pieces, the bones were being hammered, I did not understand what was happening. [48]

Would an uninformed individual in a situation like that one contemplate suicide? Why not? Instead of "enlightenment" he seems to be getting the depths of hell itself.

THE ENEMY WITHIN

TM is designed to help the meditator to turn inwards 180 degrees. [49] He is to go within himself to "pure awareness," "to the divine," "to Brahman." Supposedly, very good things are found deeply hidden within the human being, and the contact with these things will have a beneficial effect on the life led by the subject.

Up to a point this is possibly true. People who have little knowledge of themselves perhaps ought to get better in touch with who they really are.

But TM seems like too much of a good thing.

The total absorption of oneself with oneself has the effect of stripping away psychological defense mechanisms to look straight at what lies within. It is not always the pretty picture the guru assumes it will be.

LSD classically has the effect of ripping away facades and giving people nakedly honest pictures of their insides. They get very frightened, and depressed, and sometimes go off the deep end. People don't seem to be designed to handle everything that may lie deeply within themselves.

Biblically, one doesn't find God by going within oneself. One finds one's true nature, but the true nature of men and God are surely different. Jesus was very plain:

> For from within, out of the heart of men proceed the evil thoughts, and fornications, thefts, murders, adulteries, deeds of coveting and wickedness, as well as deceit, sensuality, envy, slander, arrogance and foolishness. All these things proceed from within and defile the man.'' (Matt. 7:21-23)

That gives a pretty good picture of the unregenerated man within, at least according to God. It would be difficult for anyone to confuse that character with God Himself.

It is not, of course, that we must hide from ourselves to make it through life, but that the mechanisms of the mind are designed to ''file away'' some material that is not helpful to the daily business of living. No one could run a profitable business in which the boss was to go through every file every day and meditate upon the contents. But the TM experience involves digging deeply within, where the mental mechanism itself has decided to file counter-productive material. This is to be done on a steady basis until enlightenment, which may fairly be described in our analogy as the day of bankruptcy when the business fails because of the inattention of the boss.

Morbid, unproductive, regressive states of mind can be

called forth by the turning within, resulting in self-glorification or hatred and destructiveness.[50] This sort of mysticism is an aberrant form of behavior, posing grave dangers for the average meditator, to say nothing of the uninformed seeker who just took up TM to help him relax.

The searching of the unconscious mind, to utilize western terms for a moment, under the care of a skilled professional psychotherapist can be a healthful exercise, if done properly. Knowing oneself in that sense is beneficial. But western psychotherapy, experimentally proved and tested over a broad spectrum of personalities for many years, is not to be compared with this treatment of the utterly uninformed by, as is so often the case in TM, the incompletely prepared.

DON'T BITE

The New Yorker magazine reviewed the frightening movie "Jaws" in two words—"Don't bite." That's pretty much what we wish to say about TM at this point.

Don't experiment with it, don't "try it on for size." Hinduism in all of its varieties has been tried for millenia with singularly unsuccessful results. This is admitted even by Indian gurus and yogis.[51] The sages of this religion have given the world much to ponder, but meditating on it in two sessions per day, as we have seen, is no way to go about it.

In this 20th century we have developed testing techniques to see how religions work and why people do what they do under this or that religious influence. Our psychology is up to date with the Maharishi's theories, and much beyond them. The evidence is clear that TM can be bad for you.

With apologies to Howling Wolf, we don't think anyone should court schizophrenia regardless of how heavenly its description by those who've been there. We think God is not found within your unconscious mind and not found by banging your head against a wall. If your family and friends tell you you're crazy, you ought to look into that, not feel superior about it in the Hindu way.

We have enough situations in life that drive people half nuts now without going out to purchase new ones. Our psychological survey in this chapter of TM's potential hazards simply arrives back at the same point as we would with drugs, with sensory deprivation, and with true schizophrenia. [52] There is a price attached to mental aberrations and it is a high one. Take care.

We could go on to list other maladies caused by TM, and we could document those as we have carefully documented all of our evidence thus far. Suffice it to say that a brief summary will give the picture. Consider carefully these certified TM phenomena: demon possession (Appendix Two), epileptic seizures, hallucinations, blackouts up to twenty hours, eyesight problems, extreme stomach cramps, mental confusion, sexual licentiousness, severe nightmares, anti-social behavior, the re-occurence of serious psychosomatic symptoms previously under control, *i.e.,* bleeding ulcer and depression requiring psychiatric care and medication.[53] Simple oxygen deprivation during meditation may also have extremely serious consequences, and it occurs twice a day with every practicing meditator, some of whom have had their breathing rates drop to 4 breaths per minute or even stop altogether![54] Maharishi says colorfully that TM leads to ''a state of extremely delicate breath where the breath could be said to be flowing and yet not flowing.[55]'' A lovely and very eastern characterization of what is commonly known as suffocating.

The Final Report of The Stanford Research Institute on Transcendental Meditation contains a closing statement that should be circulated very widely, as widely as the guru has circulated his publicity:

> Finally, the possibility of long-term deleterious effects from the practice of TM, especially in unstable individuals, should be investigated.[56]

FOOTNOTES: CHAPTER FIVE

Introductory quotations: *TM: Overcoming Stress and Discovering Inner Energy*, p. 149; *London Times*, June 30, 1973; John White, ed., *The Highest State of Consciousness*, p. 459; *On the Bhagavad Gita*, p. 412; John White, ed., *Frontiers of Consciousness*, p. 65; Charles Tart, ed., *Altered States of Consciousness*, p. 16; *Transcendental Meditation*, p. 223.

1. G. Ray Jordan, Jr., "LSD and Mystical Experience," in John White, ed., *The Highest State of Consciousness* (Anchor, 1972), p. 280.

2. Marilyn Ferguson, *The Brain Revolution* (Bantam, 1975), p. 176; WGBH-TV *op. cit.*, (see Notes Chapter Two).

3. White, *Everything You Want to Know About TM*, pp. 80-81.

4. Maharishi, *Transcendental Meditation*, p. 279.

5. Encyclopedia Britannica articles on hypnosis and auto-hypnosis; Arthur J. Deikman, "Experimental Meditation" in Charles Tart, ed., *Altered States of Consciousness*, pp. 218-21.

6. Bloomfield, *TM: Overcoming Stress*, Chart 1.

7. White, *Everything You Want to Know . . .*, pp. 31-2, 94, with Gopi Krishna, *The Awakening of Kundalini* (Dutton, 1975), p. 57; Shah, *op. cit.*, p. 109; Dr. Mike Miller, UCLA Neuro-psychiatric Institute; Dr. David Coddon, *U.S. News and World Report*, Sept. 15, 1975, p. 54; M.G. Satyanadham, Head, Dept. English, Government Degree College, "Transcendental Meditation," *Evangelical Student*, P.O. Box 1030, 5e Millers Road, Madras, 600010, India, p. 26.

8. Rammurti S. Mishra, *Fundamentals of Yoga* (Anchor, 1974), p. 2; Jean Houston, Robert E.L. Masters, "The Experimental Induction of Religious Type Experiences," in John White, ed., *The Highest State of Consciousness*, p. 316; Simeon Edmunds, *Hypnosis and Psychic Powers* (1972).

9. "Transpersonal Potentialities of Deep Hypnosis," *Journal of Transpersonal Psychology*, pp. 27-40, #1, 1970.

10. "Implications of LSD and Experimental Mysticism," *Journal of Transpersonal Psychology*, Fall, 1969, p. 84.

11. Jordan, *op. cit.*, p. 279; Timothy Leary, "The Religious Experience: Its Production and Interpretation," in E.F. Heenan, ed., *Mystery, Magic and Miracle* (Prentice Hall, 1973).

12. Panke, *op. cit.*, p. 75.

13. Maharishi, *On the Bhagavad Gita*, p. 464.

14. Jordan, *op. cit.*, p. 287; Heenan, *op. cit.*, p. 45.

15. *Meditations of Maharishi*, p. 90.

16. Maharishi, *Gita*, p. 422; Maharishi, *Transcendental Meditation*, pp. 103, 124.

17. C.B. Purdom (Sheriar Press, 1971), p. 137.

18. *Ibid.*, p. 138.

19. *Ibid.*, pp. 20-54.

20. Ken Wapnick, "Mysticism and Schizophrenia," *Journal of Transpersonal Psychology*, Fall, 1969.

21. *Ibid.*, p. 49; William Johnston, *Silent Music, the Science of Meditation* (Harper & Row, 1975), p. 28.

22. *The Varieties of Religious Experience* (Mentor, 1958), p. 326.

23. Johnston, *op. cit.*, p. 95.

24. Transcript of personal interview conducted by Dave Haddon, SCP, P.O. Box 4308, Berkeley, CA, partially published in *Right On*, Nov. 1975, same address.

25. Maharishi, *On the Bhagavad Gita*, p. 434.

26. (Delta, 1970), p. 222.

27. *Everything You Want to Know About TM*, p. 34.

28. Personal correspondence with John Parks.

29. p. 297.

30. Personal correspondence with Dr. Miller.

31. *On the Bhagavad Gita*, p. 389; Campbell, *op. cit.*, p. 69.

32. Brad Steiger, Paul Twitchell, *In My Soul I Am Free* (Zebra, 1975), pp. 11-12.

33. Personal correspondence with Mr. Ashman.

34. Taped interview from SCP, P.O. Box 4308, Berkeley, CA, published in *Right On*, Nov. 1975, same address.

35. June 30, 1973.

36. Maharishi, *Gita*, pp. 173, 320, 369, 403, 433-4; *Transcendental Meditation*, pp. 53, 55.

37. *Gita*, pp. 169, 393-4, 404; *Transcendental Meditation*, pp. 45-6, 118; *Meditations*, pp. 100-1.

38. *Transcendental Meditation*, p. 45.

39. Johnston, *op. cit.*, pp. 33-41; Elmer and Alyce Green, "Voluntary Control of Internal States: Psychological and Physiological," *Journal of Transpersonal Psychology*, pp. 10-14; Bloomfield, *op. cit.*, Chart 5 (1-8).

40. *Astral Doorways* (Samuel Weiser, 1975), p. 98.

41. *Time*, Oct. 13, 1975, p. 74.

42. *Seven Schools of Yoga*, pp. 28-9.

43. Johnston, *op. cit.*, pp. 115-117; Daniel Goleman, "Meditation as Meta-Therapy: Hypothesis Toward a Proposed Fifth State of Consciousness," *Journal of Transpersonal Psychology*, #1, 1971, p. 14, cf. JTP #2 1971, C.T. Tart, "A Psychologist's Experience with Transcendental Meditation," note p. 137.

44. This was the experience of one ex-meditator who prefers to remain unnamed cf. Note 53, *Literature Review*, p. 41.

45. Several ex-teachers and meditators have told me that given the right conditions it would not surprise them that violently hostile acts could be committed from unstressing.

46. Goleman, *loc. cit.*, pp. 10-11.

47. *loc. cit.*, pp. 93, 28. Johnston, *loc. cit.*, pp. 93, 28.

48. Shree Purshit Swami, *Aphorisms of Yoga* (London: Faber and Faber, 1973), pp. 57-8.

49. *Meditations*, p. 103.

50. Johnston, *op. cit.*, p. 95, 100-1.

51. Rieker, *op. cit.*, p. 190; Krishna, *op. cit.*, p. 81.

52. There may also be a similarity to epileptic states, cf. Campbell, *op. cit.*, pp. 11, 130-1, and Ferguson, *op. cit.*, pp. 180-1; *Meditations*, pp. 100-1, 178-83; *Gita*, pp. 144, 164, 305, 362-3, 404, 422, 464, 486; *Transcendental Meditation*, pp. 41-53, 103, 194-5, 236, 246, 282, 287-8.

53. Otis, *The Psychology of Meditation: Some Psychological Changes*, pp. 16-17; *The Psychobiology of Transcendental Meditation: A Literature Review*, pp. 33-47, both from SRI; Ferguson, *op. cit.*, pp. 70-1, 171-81 with Campbell, *op. cit.*, p. 11 with Greg Randolph Interview; Blair, *Journal of Transpersonal Psychology*, #1, 1970, p. 65; Benson, *op. cit.*, pp. 120-1; Naranjo and Ornstein, *op. cit.*, p. 166; Kroll, *London Times*, June 30, 1973, "The Dangers of Transcendental Meditation;" The *London Times* Education Supplement, May 17, 1974 Sri Krishna Prem, *The Yoga of the Bhagavad Gita* (Penguin, 1973), p. 53; personal correspondence.

54. The *Times* educational Supplement, May 17, 1974; *Psychology Today*, April 1974, p. 44; Campbell, *op. cit.*, p. 51; Wood, *Seven Schools of Yoga*, pp. 27-8; White, *Everything You Want to know About TM*, p. 20; Lawrence, *op. cit.*, pp. 220-221; *Transcendental Meditation*, pp. 195, 197, 207; *Gita*, p. 173.

55. *Transcendental Meditation*, p. 195.

56. *The Psychobiology of Transcendental Meditation: A Literature Review*, p. 47. cf. Chapter Two Notes 11, 16.

"Anyone with the slightest experience of meditation knows about the uprising of the unconscious and the possible resultant turmoil, to say nothing of the increased psychic power meditation brings. All this could have the greatest social consequences if meditation becomes widespread."

William Johnston

"If everyone lived as I do, how would the world go on?"

Recluse Baba Kuhi

"The snake (Kundalini yoga) will capture *some* people, *more* people. As New York begins to stink and go begging like Calcutta, the snake will insinuate itself into a few anxious bellies."

Dr. Colin Campbell

"One who is not conducted by false ego and whose intelligence is not entangled, even killing in this world, he is not killing; and neither is he bound by such action."

Krishna, Bhagavad Gita, 18:17

"The man who knows me as I am loses nothing whatever he does. Even if he kills his mother or his father, even if he steals or procures an abortion; for whatever evil he does, he does not blanch if he knows me as I am."

Indra, an incarnation of Brahman

"Whatever is necessary, you do it. When somebody needs to be killed, there's no wrong. You do it, and then you move on . . . you kill whoever gets in your way. That is us."

Sandra Good, one of the "Manson girls"

"You really have to have a lot of love in your heart to do what I did to (Sharon) Tate."

Susan Atkins, one of the "Manson girls"

"Can there be grief in the mind of a wise man either for the living or for the dead?"

Maharishi

"You know that my deadly nightmare is to feel that I am lost in this ocean of blood, coming from innumerable victims."

Lenin

CHAPTER SIX

THE MANSON FACTOR

TM is antisocial. It runs very seriously against the grain of virtually all human society in its insistence that the real world, its people and events, are not real after all, and only Brahman exists. [1]

It is difficult to appreciate what incredible extremes of antisocial behavior result from such a way of looking at life, from the "spacey" detachment of the seasoned meditator to the casually murderous philosophy of Charles Manson. One's philosophy of life, however, deeply determines one's philosophy of death, and, as we shall see, the Hindu way of looking at life and death is responsible for stupefying excesses of antisocial behavior, including Manson's.[2]

Manson boasted of committing some 35 murders, [3] including his celebrated execution of Sharon Tate and friends. Since Manson was a glibly clever talker and held sway over any number of disciples, people became interested in how this seemingly intelligent small-time dictator justified his crimes. Interviews were held and books written as Manson calmly explained his schemes for a future improved society and his methods for contributing to it. People were stunned.

Prosecutor Vincent Bugliosi wrote of Manson, "I do believe that if Manson had the opportunity, he would have become another Hitler. I can't conceive of his stopping short of murdering huge masses of people."[4] Manson said, "Hitler had the best answer to everything."[5]

Manson believed in a coming super race of people and spoke in Hindu terms about Hitler. He said that Hitler "was a tuned-in guy who had leveled the karma of the Jews.[6]" He believed the philosophy of Nietzsche where it concerned the "master race," and he saw himself as some kind of crusader working toward achieving the new age. He believed that mass murder was only right—some are fit and some are unfit for the coming system—that's the law of evolution.

THE FOLLY OF EVOLUTION

Here are echoes of Biblical prophecy for the end times in general with its ever-coming occult "Age of Enlightenment," and Maharishi in particular. Remember the guru's evolutionary assessment of his own new age: "There has not been and there will not be a place for the unfit. The fit will lead, and if the unfit are not coming along there is no place for them.[7]"

Few people seem to be aware of the very negative impact, historically, of evolutionary thinking—not to mention the fact that the general theory of evolution is really philosophy, not science and that the scientific *facts* point to creation, not evolution. Scholarly books such as Dr. Coppedges *Evolution: Possible or impossible?* , Dr. Wysong's *The Creation-Evolution controversy*, Dr. Shute's *Flaws in the Theory of Evolution*, and Wilder-Smith's *The Creation of Life, A Cybernetic Approach to Evolution*, (Smith has three doctorates in science) as well as dozens of others show that not only has evolution not occurred, its very occurrence is a complete impossibility. Since there are only two possible answers to the origin of life, and as Dr. Wysong clearly shows, "there is no scientific evidence for evolution" (p. 421) creation by God is the only logical alternative. Wyson demonstrates that the faith of the evolutionist is a blind faith in the clearly impossible:

Evolution requires plenty of faith: a faith in L-proteins that defy chance formation; a faith in the formation of DNA codes which if generated spontaneously would spell only pandamonium; a faith in a primitive environment that in reality would fiendishly devour any chemical precursors to life; a faith in (origin of life) experiments that prove nothing but the need for intelligence in the beginning; a faith in a primitive ocean that would not thicken but would hopelessly dilute chemicals; a faith in natural laws including the laws of thermodynamics and biogenesis that actually deny the possibility for the spontaneous generation of life; a faith in future scientific revelations that when realized always seem to present more dilemmas to the evolutionist; faith in probabilities that treasonously tell two stories—one denying evolution, the other confirming the creator; faith in transformations that remain fixed; faith in mutations and natural selection that add to a double negative for evolution; faith in fossils that embarrassingly show fixity through time, regular absence of transitional forms and striking testimony to a world-wide water deluge; a faith in time which proves to only promote degradation in the absence of mind; and faith in reductionism that ends up reducing the materialist's arguments to zero and forcing the need to invoke a supernatural creator." "True one is still free to believe in evolution but it appears he must simply give up math, physics, chemistry, thermodynamics, etc., to keep the faith.[8]

Since evolution has not occurred—since there are no signs of it, God obviously hasn't used the process to create man. To associate God with such a cruel, haphazard unbiblical method is to impugn His character (Gen. 1:31; Rom. 5:12—could God pronounce "very good" millions of years of struggle, death, decay, and evolutionary misfits?) Evolution is one-tenth bad science and nine tenths bad philosophy.

THE DEATH OF LIFE

Where Manson and the guru connect most noticeably is in their shared concept that death is of little importance. To Manson there was no death at all. Death was merely some sort of change in status, "no more important than eating an ice cream cone,[9]" and certainly nothing to grieve over. With Maharishi, truly wise men grieve over nothing, not even the death of those close to them, since everything is Brahman and Brahman cannot die.[10] The guru concedes that people's bodies "die"—but this is of no importance because their bodies are not real anyway. The guru, like Manson, feels that death is a natural event "about which one should not feel much concern...no one should grieve over the death of another.[11]"

We noted in the last chapter the lack of concern by brother Lutes of the TM movement over suicide statistics among the TM teachers. Lutes was certain that those who passed on would be attended personally, and given new mantras (for a new sort of society?) by the honored Guru Dev.

The familiar chords of death-is-not-important, a-New-Age-is-dawning, follow-our-leader-no-matter-what, ring through cultic worship of every kind and have the distinct effect of making ordinary people into deeply committed crusaders after some utopian-styled cause. That Hitler and his henchmen were maniacs was clear to see, but that they galvanized an entire nation into doing their infamous bidding was downright amazing, and only proves the power of such "new-age" systems. Naturally Hitler did not begin his career by announcing the negatives of his system; he could hardly have gained followers telling ordinary people that they would have to do a lot of inconvenient killing to get to the new order. Instead he bragged of a new system where his select people would prevail and the whole world would be a better place. Hitler was a student of eastern mysticism and the occult; his private library was replete with such materials. He was also a man occassionally described as "possessed" and may have derived his "superior race" ideas from experiencing the "higher consciousness" of eastern mysticism or drugs.[12]

Interestingly, those people he found to be the least fit for his system were the chosen people of the Bible. The Jewish karma, whatever that is, is still intact and the leader of the Third Reich is gone, but there is always another leader and another "new age."

We don't mean to imply that Maharishi is another Manson or another Hitler, of course. But he difinitely *is* another leader with a new-age philosophy and many of the same ideas about life and death, superiority and inferiority among people, and unswerving devotion to the cause. As to whether his meditation system will lead people to the wretched excesses of those past self-styled utopians, time will tell. Our concern here is that it can definitely lead people to deeply antisocial behavior affecting the whole fabric of a society in proportion to the number of devotees.

STRANGE SIMILARITIES

It is a cause of concern that there are similarities in both the mental states and the changes in personality and world view of those who use psychedelic drugs, those who engage in occult-mystical experiences, the insane, and the Hindu mystics. We have already established TM's link with the latter. Found in them all are the dissolution of the ego or personality, the divine "oneness" with everything, the indifferent acceptance of life and death, the breakdown of reality, etc.[13] According to ex-family members, Manson's control over others was exerted very gradually through having them lose their individual egos. This loss allowed them to experience the oneness of everything. He talked about love and how you had to surrender yourself to it. "Only by ceasing to exist as an individual ego could you become one with all things," he said.[14] Hitler used the same techniques to whip up the crowds' emotions to support him.[15] Manson's family was taught to have a passive and amoral acceptance of the events of life and death. The world was simply god's imagination; then it was simply *their* imagination. They had to give up their egos, their "I" and also give up thinking. They were not to think, and they were never to question Charlie.[16] In TM, you are never to question Maharishi, ("The Yogi, his word is law").[17] TM leads to a passive acceptance of life and death events, the dissolution of the ego, an unreal world, the unity experience ...everything Manson used to gain control over his "blood-thirsty robots." It is noteworthy that ex-family member Paul Watkins said Manson used LSD trips and *Scientology processing* to go deep into the mind (another TM feat) and take out all moral inhibitions so they could wantonly murder.[18] Bugliosi, too, notes that Manson used Scientology techniques to control and program his followers.[19] (In passing we should mention that Scientology and its methods are both immoral and dangerous.)[20] The experience of pantheism and ego-dissolution is extremely deceptive and is so contraty to the Christian world view it can easily be viewed as the work of Satan.

THE GOOD LIFE

With Maharishi you can do no wrong.

We can follow the guru's reasoning right from his dismissal of the seriousness of death and killing through to his implication that anyone faithfully practicing TM is always pure, always in the right.

Maharishi admires a certain story in the Bhagavad Gita centered on a battlefield. Supposedly Brahman was incarnated as Krishna in order to counsel a certain soldier, Arjuna, who had relatives in the opposing army. Arjuna was squeamish about fighting against his own kin but Krishna straightened him out in the Hindu way. Arjuna would incur a great sin if he does 'not' kill his own relatives because, after all, life is only temporary, unreal and of no consequence. If Arjuna is going to stand there and act as if the death of his family has some sort of real meaning he will merely betray his own ignorance of truth.[21] It is more important for Arjuna to obey his caste duty as a warrior and to go out there and kill. This will enhance the evolution of all creatures.[22] Arjuna must cooperate with the doctrine.

Maharishi steps carefully in his ancient Master's footsteps in his commentary on the Bhagavad Gita:

> Do not give importance to the consideration of the fleeting and impermanent phases of life. Rise to the understanding that the permanent Reality of existence will continue to be...the present phenomenal phase of existence [that is, real life as we see it] is seen to have no permanent significance.

The TM peacemaker says:

> The event of war is a natural phenomenon...
> To rise to the call of a war to establish righteousness is

to respond to the cosmic purpose, the will of God.[23]

And here comes the part we were telling you about. Maharishi now goes from the fact that life and death are not real to the astounding fact that those practicing TM rise above any considerations of right and wrong! His point is that when the meditator rises to the level of the Absolute via TM, every action done by the meditator comes from the Absolute and is thus perfectly in tune with nature. The consummate TM devotee is, in the words of the guru, "above the realms of right and wrong, his actions are quite naturally right actions.[24] "'This is a state of life where no wrong action is possible . . .'" "A man in cosmic consciousness cannot, in principle, be judged by what he does.[25]"

THE MANSON CONNECTION

We can now very directly compare Manson's philosophy concerning the irrelevance of standards of right and wrong with Maharishi's. Manson's beliefs on this issue were told by his acquaintance of several years, Gregg Jakobson, who was questioned by prosecutor Bugliosi:

Q. What did Manson say, if anything, about right and wrong?
A. He believed you could do no wrong, no bad. Everything was good. Whatever you do is what you are supposed to do; you are following your own Karma.

At this point Bugliosi comments, "The philosophical mosaic began taking shape. The man I was seeking to convict had no moral boundaries. It was not that he was immoral, but totally *amoral*. And such a person is always dangerous."

135

Q. Did he say it was wrong to kill a human being?
A. He said it was not.
Q. What was Manson's philosophy regarding death?
A. There was no death, to Charlie's way of thinking. Death was only a change. The soul or spirit can't die...that's what we used to argue all the time...[26]

We can well take the very next sentence from Maharishi:

Death as such only causes a temporary pause in the process of evolution...(and) is no real danger to life.[27]

The guru's further commentary on the counsel of Krishna to the hesitant warrior Arjuna is relevant:

One thing was deep-rooted in Arjuna's mind: the feeling that his sharp arrows would pierce and mutilate the bodies of those he held dear and slay them. That is why the Lord (Krishna) begins by making him understand that their existence would not, in any real sense, be destroyed by his weapons. Reality is one, omnipresent, devoid of any duality, without components—that is why It cannot be slain. The body is composed of different parts—that is why it can be slain.... His aim is to show Arjuna that the Self, being transcendental, remains ever untouched by anything in this relative field.[28]

However Arjuna felt about this soothing philosophy, the "sharp-arrows-[that]-would-pierce-and-mutilate" part was not lost on Charles Manson. Bugliosi reports on how the latter-day karma lover dealt with his victims:

136

Voytek Frykowski: shot twice, hit over the head 13 times...stabbed 51 times.

Rosemary LaBianca: forty-one knife wounds.

Leno LaBianca: 12 knife wounds, punctured with a fork 7 times, a knife in his throat, a fork in his stomach, and, on the wall, in his own blood, DEATH TO PIGS.[29]

Krishna would have been proud.

Krishna says, "Even if a devotee commits the most abominable actions he is to be considered saintly because he is properly situated.[30]" (i.e., regarding life and death)

Perhaps Manson had achieved a very high level of consciousness, and we are misunderstanding his acts of love. After all, as Maharishi says of Arjuna:

(He has to) attain a state of consciousness which will justify any action of his and will allow him even to kill in love, in support of the purpose of evolution.[31]

THE NON-TM UNFORTUNATES

In spite of the excesses found in the logical extension of Maharishi's beliefs, the guru is very tough on non-meditators. While his own antisocial philosophy is open to exploitation and evil on the level of Charles Manson, he soundly condemns those who will not take part. According to the guru's own writings, those who have not reached the state of god-realization are:

> The ignorant, the unfit, abnormal, out of touch with reality, selfish, pitiable, thieves, slaves, destructive, unstable, incapable of love, retarders of the welfare of others, and undeserving to be called human.[32]

Were it not for the term "pitiable" one would think the gentle Maharishi lacks compassion. "Blessed are those who speak sweet words," he says.[33]

WHO WAS I?

The belief in reincarnation, central to the Hindu religion, and the closely related concept of death as "a temporary pause in the process of evolution," as the guru puts it, has caused India some real social problems.

We have already looked briefly at Hindu society, but in this chapter on the antisocial implications of the TM philosophy we might profit by a closer examination of Maharishsi's thoughts at work. Our modern guru is the descendant of the same schools of thought that constructed the caste system, the worship of animals, the conviction that life is unreal and the modern meditation program. India today is the ultimate application of this kind of thinking. We might call it the future of TM, as TM is a much more intensive immersion into Hinduism than the average person suspects.

We are not trying to connect things that don't go together. It should be clearly understood that Maharishi is a devout believer in reincarnation and karma, and a supporter of the caste system, with all of its cruelties by western standards. The peace-promoting guru who looks serenely out from the posters is able to stomach the starvation of millions with the same blithe unconcern as he shows over the death of Arjuna's relatives.[34] He finds nothing wrong in India, as he finds nothing wrong anywhere else, looking down from his elevated position of god-realization. Anyway, when all is said and done in unity consciousness, India's troubles *are* not real and don't exist.

To those of us who have not adopted Maharishi's outlook, it seems tragic that people should live in poverty, disease and filth, and die of starvation, leaving their decimated bodies to be collected each evening by passing trucks in the streets of the largest cities in India. For these unfortunate ones, their trouble really started long ago with the founding of the doctrine of reincarnation.

According to reincarnation we go on from life to life, progressing or regressing according to the karma we accumulate in each life. Karma repays us in the next life for the good or evil we have done in the present one. If we are good, we progress to better circumstances in the next life; if we are evil, we get demoted, even to the status of becoming an animal in the next life.

This system, which, on the surface, may seem just, has led to some sickeningly unjust manifestations in India today. The impoverished underfed multitudes are thought of as simply receiving just retribution for evil they have done in a previous life. Helping to feed them or get them out of their hopeless circumstances would be interfering with their karma and thus a religious violation, even sinful. They are getting their just deserts, and one must not interfere with the workings of the gods. They are not only doomed by karma, but by the caste system as well that declares most of these unfortunates to be ''Untouchables,'' and thus not to be helped by those of higher caste.

So they just rot away and die, and the trucks come by and get them out of the way of the better folks.

Inexplicably, however, animals, who ought to be very low on the reincarnation scale, are fed while the people starve. There is a religious respect for the animal kingdom, and out-and-out worship of cattle, in Hinduism. Maharishi subscribes to the doctrine of *ahimsa*,[35] which prescribes non-violence to all living creatures but seems to work mostly to the advantage of the lower creatures. ''The Being of an evolved man and that of the animals is the same,[36]'' says the guru, in support of his concept that the animals and people are of the same essence.

Manson shared this ironic respect for animals. He was never troubled by his picturesque killings of people but became deeply upset over the killing of any other living thing, even a bug or a flower.[37]

Maharishi teaches that, ''The form of the cow and the form of the dog fail to blind [the God-realized man] to the oneness of the Self, which is the same in both. Although he sees a cow and a dog, his Self is established in the being of the cow and the Being of the dog, which is his own Being.[38]''

ALL HAIL SAINT RAT, SAINT SNAKE AND LORD COW

This is serious. People worship rats in parts of India. And the rats get better treatment than the people themselves!

Today in India there are some 2.4 *billion* rats, outnumbering the people 5 to 1, and they consume enough grain annually to feed at least 15 million people, India's annual growth rate. [39]

Rat worship seems unbelievable to western minds, but in Bilaner, in Rajasthan, there is a temple devoted exclusively to rat worship and it is overrun with thousands of the destructive, disease-spreading creatures. [40] In Calcutta, a relatively modern city, the main street boasts a rat park where rats cavort and play as the passers-by approve. In one year Bombay suffered 58,000 cases of rat bites, [41] which are extremely dangerous whatever one's religion. The rats seem not to appreciate the special attention and worship they receive. Or perhaps they are typical Hindu gods, tormenting their own worshippers with inattention and constant danger of suffering and death. No wonder that Masters and Houston estimate that 90% of India's holy men are on hemp and various other drugs. [42]

Monkeys and snakes are also worshipped in India, and particularly cows, as we have noted. Virtually every animal is sacred in some way. The snakes have a great deal to do with occult worship, and maybe a tiny bit with Genesis. As author Idries Shah notes, "In India today, snake-worship is rife . . . snakes bring good fortune, guard souls and hidden treasures, form the outlet for occult utterances. [43]" The Hindus have mistaken the Biblical character of the snake as completely as the Biblical character of God. Even little children play with deadly cobras in the Indian households. [44]

But the real sacred cow is the sacred cow. If the Indians stuck to rats and snakes their food problem might not be what it is today, but they choose to worship and to protect one of the heartiest creatures with one of the biggest appetites on land. And naturally they never partake of its flesh for food.

The homage paid to the cow in India is almost unimaginable, and to western minds perhaps one of the strangest of religious sacraments:

The Artharva Veda repeatedly deprecates cow-killing as 'the most heinous of crimes.' All that kill, eat or permit the slaughter of cows rot in hell for as many years as there are hairs on the body of the cow slain. Capital punishment was prescribed for those who either stole, hurt or killed a cow.... Even cows' urine and dung are sacred to the Brahmins. 'All its excreta are hallowed. Not a particle ought to be thrown away as impure (today certain yogis line their huts daily with fresh cow dung. Numerous zealots sip the urine.[45]) On the contrary, the water it ejects ought to be preserved as the best of holy waters.... Any spot which a cow has condescended to honour with the sacred deposit of her excrement is forever afterwards consecrated ground.' Sprinkled on a sinner, the urine 'converts him into a saint.[46]'

This perverse and unsanitary 'baptism' rather shows the extremes of paganism found at the logical extension of such strange initial religious concepts as the ancient Hindu Masters taught. This seems a long way from TM, at least as it is advertised, but then TM is only beginning in the west. Being a branch of the sick tree of Hinduism it may well show the same fruits as time goes by.

THE GODDESS OF SMALLPOX

The incredible indifference toward even a killer like smallpox, endemic to India today, illustrates the end result of masses of people becoming convinced that life and all of its parts are unreal and meaningless. Some readers will not believe that the Hindus have a goddess of smallpox, but her name is Shitala and her temples are as legion as her ugly legacy to the people itself.

Like the other indifferent Hindu gods, Shitala has made life very hard for her worshipers. While the western nations have eradicated her disease, septic Hindu customs continue to provide its best breeding ground. Time magazine reported the horrible death toll of a recent Indian smallpox epidemic: 100,000 afflicted, with at least 20,000 dead. But many of the Indian people in the backward states—Bihar, for example, with sixty million terribly misguided souls—refuse available vaccine! They "would sooner travel 100 miles to a temple of Shitala to pray to her to spare their children than report to the nearest vaccination center a few miles away.[47]"

It should be stressed that we do not report such a horror story for the purpose of deprecating the Indian people or their deplorable circumstances of poverty and lack of modern technology. But we do deprecate the debilitating paganism which teaches that God will be cruel and will slaughter the people wholesale as He pleases, and that there is no possible answer to this situation except blanking the mind. The social conditions of India, like the social conditions in the west, come about largely as a result of how the people think spiritually. When the people at large think life can be improved, nature confronted successfully and God reached by love, rather than oblivion, the society shows it. When God is the same as nature, and present circumstances are the result of karma, life simply overwhelms helpless people.

We feel strongly that the Hindu customs and traditions amount to a true enmity toward God, with the expected results.

THE UNSOCIAL SET?

Now social indifference is not supposed to happen among TM meditators. These are people of action, utilizing modern techniques and taking full advantage of the blessings of Brahman's supervision of all of their social actions.

Yet, Maharishi teaches a straight line of Hindu indifference to life, complete with the TM goal of reaching the state of total unconcern and total uninvolvement with one's own actions and in a way, their consequences.[48] The accomplished meditator realizes that he is not the author of his own actions, which are merely a matter of Brahman's sport or play.[49] The realm of action does not belong to true life and reality for the one practicing TM, who has left all that behind.[50]

TM theory must not be applied, according to the guru, by those who aren't initiated meditators (called ''the ignorant''), because this may lead them to a philosophy of indifference, amorality (Manson) and a refusal to take responsibility for one's actions. Knowledge and truth, says this particular line, are found only in experiencing higher states of consciousness. Those who fail to achieve higher consciousness will thus misinterpret the Master.[51]

This technique (''If you see a bad apple I didn't grow it'') protects Maharishi from the very evils of his own system. If his initiates start to act like so many robot Hindus, it can always be said that ''They didn't really understand. They are ignorant.'' Maharishi even condemns just the sort of social indifference his own system ultimately creates, seeking the way out.

But the TM meditator becomes automatically, by the very doctrine of the cult, separated from society. It is not just that he meditates; we all meditate about things. It is his intensive training in the principles of the Hinduism we have been looking at which creates the antisocial effect. Listen to

Maharishi's teaching on the level of meditator involvement in society:

Because his self is fixed in the universal Self, there is nothing he could gain from another. His Self is uninvolved in every way—it is uninvolved with activity and it is uninvolved with the *selves* of individual beings. His own Self is the Self of all beings.[52]

This world of joys and sorrows, of man's great enterprise and ambition, is for them like a world of dolls and toys with which children play and amuse themselves. Toys are a great source of excitement for children, but grown-ups remain untouched by them.[53]

THE FRUIT OF INDIFFERENCE

Maharishi says plainly, as part of the above teaching, that those in cosmic consciousness are ''far above the boundaries of any social bond or obligation.'' The guru argues that the meditator neither rejoices nor recoils over any good or evil, and that ''indifference is the weapon to be used against any negative situation in life.[54]'' The example is given of a wise man who saw only good in everything, and when he was shown a rotting dog carcass in the street he noticed only the shining white teeth of the dog.[55]

We only wish it were that easy. But when evil is ignored evil flourishes, as in India. The overall decay of any society is greatly aided by the steady obliviousness toward greater and greater evils among the people, until what was once criminal becomes finally acceptable and even desirable. The dead dog's teeth still bite.

Those who practice TM, according to Maharishi, are those who see life as the sport and drama of the Divine ''while they themselves remain uninvolved.[56]'' Somehow these oblivious ones are going to usher in the Age of Enlightenment.

The position of the totally committed Hinduistic meditator is summed up by R. Zaehner, author of *Zen, Drugs, and Mysticism*:

The Absolute (Brahman or the universal Self) is wholly indifferent to what goes on in the world. 'He does not speak and has no care.' 'He neither increases by good works, nor does he diminish by evil ones.' Similarly in the case of the man who has realized that in the ground of his being he is identical with the Absolute, these two thoughts do not occur to him—'So I have done evil' or 'So I have done what is good and fair.' He shrugs them off . . . This is because, seeing the Self in himself and all things as the Self, he will be indifferent to all actions, good or evil, which take place in the phenomenal [real] world.[57]

ONWARD TO OBLIVION

The TM procedure of continually retreating to an impersonal mental state and fashioning oneself after the image of an impersonal, indifferent god does finally change ones values, as Maharishi admits.[58] Ex-meditator Allen Fox became very disenchanted with TM and his TM associates because, ''They became so self-enclosed and boring. They stopped caring about anybody or anything else.[59]''

Like the drug addicts, Indian meditators fail to even care for their physical bodies and even purposely damage themselves beyond repair. Proving that the body is insignificant and meaningless, the yogis of India, as is well known, mortify their own flesh by staring at the sun until they are blind, allowing limbs to wither through inactivity, burning themselves to death and failing to nourish themselves.[60]

Thomas notes:

> "The practice of some of these Shaivas [Shiva worshipers] emphasizes the need for torturing the flesh to elevate the soul. The Bahikathas for instance, tear their bodies with knives and daggers . . . The Aghoris feed on carrion [dead animals] and excreta, and because of their predilection for burial places are even suspected of worse things. The Kapalikas use a human skull for a drinking bowl... There are various other sects... who select forms of self-torture... while nameless sects of Shaivas organize themselves into gangs and terrorize the countryside in the name of Shiva.[61]"

Devotees of Shiva's wife, Kali, are instructed to keep a constant flow of blood at her numerous altars, lest she send epidemics and disasters into the world to slake her thirst. Even human sacrifice cannot be ruled out. The Los Angeles Times of Feb. 15, 1976, reports on the "dacoits" who also worship the death goddess Kali and travel about plundering and murdering victims in sacrifice to her.

TM instructors and meditators, as we have seen, progress even to suicide, no doubt influenced, perhaps unwittingly, by the philosophy that life and death are not real. This actually becomes a highly desirable state of spirituality, certifying to all who care to understand that the mortified one is indeed God-realized. Rather like Japan's Kamikaze pilots of World War II, they sacrifice themselves for great honor and better things to come. They gain great respect, at least among their fellows, for making the supreme obeisance.

147

It is one thing for the one practicing TM to do himself in socially, but quite another for him to spread this doctrine so that the entire society is affected. When the entire society is threatened the meditator has overstepped his rights, obviously, and surely ought to be discouraged from promulgating his strange doctrine. There are too many people, in any society, who are taken in by promises of peace and bliss.

The logical end of TM theory is reflected in India, where the obtuse Hindu doctrines hold sway and many people are emphatically, cold-bloodedly antisocial. The human being is demeaned and his dignity removed; the animals are actually placed above him; diseases flourish; the nobility of the creative human mind is made to equal nothing. People care nothing for each other or for survival itself.

As we go on to examine the personal experiences of ex-devotees of TM in the following chapter, it will be clearly seen that what we have said thus far is not merely theory. Some of our most troubling descriptions of the results of TM have been reported by accomplished meditators who have somehow found their way back to the living.

The real horror stories are yet to come.

FOOTNOTES: CHAPTER SIX

Introductory quotations: *Silent Music, The Science of Meditation*, p. 26; A. Campbell, *Seven States of Consciousness*, p. 61; *Psychology Today*, Dec. 1975, p. 104; A.C. Prabhupada, *Bhagavad Gita As It Is* (Collier, 1972), p. 303; *Kaushitaki Upanishad*, 3.1-2; Vincent Bugliosi, *Helter Skelter*, p. 624; "Charlie Manson: Portrait in Terror," Feb. 16, 1976, Channel 7, KABC-TV, Los Angeles, 11:30 p.m., description by Bugliosi; *On the Bhagavad Gita*, p. 90; *Right On*, Vol. 1, #4, p. 2, P.O. Box 4308, Berkeley, CA.

1. The end of TM teachings is indifference, nihilism, amorality and an unreal world. This is a logical derivation from Maharishi's writings: *On the Bhagavad Gita*, pp. 76, 90-107, 127-30, 142, 157, 172-5, 203, 219, 222-5, 282, 295, 321-5, 340, 426, 434; *Transcendental Meditation*, pp. 66, 72, 112, 128, 145, 147, 132-3, 150, 164-6, 201-2, 220-5, 295-6; *Meditations*, p. 51, etc.

2. Cf. Vincent Bugliosi, *Helter Skelter* (Bantam, 1975), pp. 300-301, 317.

3. Bugliosi, *op. cit.*, p. 641.

4. *Ibid.*, p. 641.

5. *Ibid.*, p. 639.

6. *Ibid.*, pp. 301, 317, 641.

7. *Inauguration of the Dawn of the Age of Enlightenment* (MIU Press, 1975), p. 47. Other support for a Hitlerian type philosophy in Maharishi's writings: pp. 25-27, 42-46, 49; *Bhagavad Gita*, pp. 167, 252, 279, 76, 376; *Transcendental Meditation*, p. 80-81, 91-3, 105, 115, 138, 154, 171, 173, 176, 201, 211, 295, 42, 48, 127, 225, 247; White, *Everything . . .*, pp. 108-28.

8. R.L. Wysong, *The Creation Evolution Controversy* (Inquiry Press, P.O. Box 1766, East Lansing, Mich. 48823) 1976, p. 419, 411.

9. Bugliosi, *op. cit.*, p. 301.

10. Maharishi, *On the Bhagavad Gita*, p. 90.

11. *Ibid.*, pp. 104, 107, 90.

12. Trevor Ravenscroft, *The Spear of Destiny* (Bantam, 1974),pp. 25-33, 49, 58, 91, 95-6, 154-68, 172-3, 243-5, 288-92; J. Angebert, *The Occult and the Third Reich* (McGraw Hill, 1975), pp. xi-xiii, 163, 194-200, 278; J.H. Brennan, *The Occult, Reich* (Signet, 1974); L. Pauwels, J. Bergier, *The Morning of the Magicians* (Avon, 1968), Part 2; W.C. Langer, *The Mind of Adolph Hitler* (Signet, 1973), p.41.

13. Charles Braden, *The Private Sea—LSD and the Search for God*, p. 22, Chs. 2-4; Chapter 5, Notes 14, 21, 1, 11; White, *The Highest State of Consciousness*, pp. 287, 459; *Chandogya Upanishad* 7.25:1; Zaehner, *Zen, Drugs and Mysticism*, p. 85, 105; John White, ed., *Frontiers of Consciousness* (Avon, 1975), p. 65.

14. Bugliosi, *op. cit.*, p. 317.

15. Angebert, *op. cit.*, p. 278.

16. "Charlie Manson: Portrait in Terror," Channel 7 (KABC) Los Angeles, 11:30 p.m., Feb. 16, 1976.

17. S.P. Swami, *Aphorisms of Yoga*, p. 53.

18. Note 15.

19. Bugliosi, *op. cit.*, p. 635.

20. L. Ron Hubbard, *The Creation of Human Ability* (Scientology Pub. 1975), p. 241; *Los Angeles Times*, June 1, 1974, Part 1, p. 20; P. Cooper, *The Scandal of Scientology* (Tower, 1971).

21. Maharishi, *On the Bhagavad Gita*, p. 81.

22. *Ibid.*, pp. 93, 105.

23. *Ibid.*, p. 108.

24. *Ibid.*, pp. 219, 130, 175, 203, 127, 142, 98-100, 108.

25. *Ibid.*, pp. 309, 174, 218, cf. 95, 96, Notes 45, 31 and 32, p. 276.

26. Bugliosi, *op. cit.*, p. 300-1.

27. *On the Bhagavad Gita*, p. 233.

28. *Ibid.*, p. 101.

29. Bugliosi, *op. cit.*, p. 327, 330h.

30. *Back to Godhead*, #55, p. 25, AC. B. Prabhupada, quoting Bhagavad Gita 9:30 (Hare Krishna magazine).

31. *On the Bhagavad Gita*, p. 76.

32. Maharishi, *Transcendental Meditation*, pp. 22, 56, 68, 83, 90-92, 102, 111, 119, 81, 136, 149, 154-5, 160, 169-70, 200-202, 279; *On the Bhagavad Gita*, pp. 140, 169-70, 202, 279, 361, cf. 76, 114, 274, 446, 449.

33. Maharishi, *Transcendental Meditation*, p. 148.

34. *Ibid.*, p. 183; *On the Bhagavad Gita*, p. 90.

35. *Ibid.*, p. 88.

36. *On the Bhagavad Gita*, p. 359.

37. Bugliosi, *op. cit.*, p. 301.

38. *On the Bhagavad Gita*, p. 359.

39. *Los Angeles Times*, August 12, 1974.

40. *Ibid.*

41. *Ibid.*

42. Charles Braden, *op. cit.*, p. 24.

43. *Oriental Magic* (Dutton, 1973), p. 4.

44. P. Thomas, *Hindu Religion, Customs, and Manners* (Bombay: Taraporevala & Co., 1960), p. 30.

45. *Ibid.*, p. 30.

46. Immanuel Velikovsky, *Worlds in Collision* (Dell, 1968), p. 190; *Ibid.*, p. 30.

47. *Time*, p. 78.

48. For documentation see: Maharishi, *On the Bhagavad Gita*, pp. 323, 325, 98, 386, 376, 142, 340, 359, 457-8, 171, 224, 174, 321, 185, 219, 92, 94, 100, 128-9, 99, 157, 212, 223, 282, 154, 373; Maharishi, *Transcendental Meditation*, pp. 46, 68, 103, 110, 113, 183, 224-5.

49. *On the Bhagavad Gita*, pp. 250, 261, 373, 416; *Transcendental Meditation*, pp. 35-6, etc.
50. *On the Bhagavad Gita*, p. 325.

51. *Ibid.*, p. 386, 224, 376, 340, 426, 257-8, 171, 184-5, 219, cf. also Note 45.

52. *Ibid.*, p. 212.

53. *Ibid.*, p. 157.

54. *Ibid.*, p. 157; *Transcendental Meditation*, p. 183.

55. *Transcendental Meditation*, pp. 224-5.

56. *On the Bhagavad Gita*, pp. 373, 416.

57. R.C. Zaehner, *Zen, Drugs and Mysticism* (Vintage, 1974), p. 162.

58. *On the Bhagavad Gita*, p. 155.

59. *Right Now*, McCalls Monthly Newsletter, Jan. 1976, p. 46.

60. Thomas, *op. cit.*, p. 26; Rieker, *op. cit.*, p. 119.

61. Thomas, *op. cit.*, pp. 26-7.

"On attaining cosmic consciousness a person's world view undergoes a radical transformation. The consensus of all mystics and sages...is that the world of normal experiences is now revealed as unreal, as phenomenal, as a mere appearance..."

Haridas Chaudhuri

"all this is nothing"

Maharishi

"Anyone who goes deeply into these (Eastern) disciplines taps mystery. Wall Street's Adam Smith, ruthlessly rational, reports in *Powers of Mind* on an invisible 'it' or presence that he feels on several kinds of meditative trips."

T. George Harris editorial

"In this state the self is lost forever;..."

Maharishi

"...in a way it was absolutely terrifying, showing that when *one thinks one's got beyond oneself, one hasn't....* I began with this marvelous sense of this cosmic gift, and then ended up with a useful sense of that one can be deceived.... It was an insight, but at the same time the most *dangerous* of errors...inasmuch as one was worshipping ones self."

Aldous Huxley, describing his experience under the sedative dilaulid, one week before his death.

"the mind in this state acts...in a rather carefree manner, which may be thought of as akin to indifference."

Maharishi

152

"When the heroin is in my blood and the blood is in my head thank God that I'm good as dead and thank your God that I'm not aware and thank God that I just don't care and I guess I just don't know, oh, and I guess I just don't know..."

The Velvet Underground, "Heroin"

CHAPTER SEVEN

SOME DISSATISFIED CUSTOMERS

At the end of five years of transcendental meditation and TM teaching Vail Hamilton, of Berkeley, didn't exactly reach God-realization. As a matter of fact she was feeling very guilty. In a taped interview with Chuck Simmons she said:

I stopped practicing it and teaching it because my conscience wouldn't let me. I realized it was a deception and I simply couldn't go along with it...something was telling me it was wrong to teach it as just a scientific technique when in reality I knew very well it was a form of Hinduism.

Vail is one of the TM drop-outs who have begun to speak up about what really goes on in the back rooms of TM. It seems that the end product of the Maharishi's system is not the bliss he promises, at least not for everybody. In this section we will discuss the testimonies of some dissatisfied customers.

Vail's higher states of consciousness apparently didn't permit her to go on with what amounted to false advertising, and the bait-and-switch technique of the TM teacher:

> I was immensely perturbed by the deception aspect of TM instruction...as an instructor I had to withhold information from the students...and then when they were sucked in, I involved them in the religious aspects of TM. [2] "

Vail didn't find God after all, and she became increasingly disturbed about the highest state of TM where her personalality was to disappear:

> This idea really bothered me—I didn't want to lose my personal identity. I wanted to remain me and wanted God to remain God and to worship Him, and TM simply was getting me further and further away from that reality...I was becoming a God unto myself and I was excusing certain behavior patterns in myself as, 'That's groovy; anything's okay because I'm meditating...' which I now know was very selfish behavior. [3]

The TM instructors' casual attitude toward greatly disturbed behavior among their number, and even schizophrenic symptoms greatly troubled Vail:

> I was at a teacher training course in 1972 in Fuji, Italy, and there was a girl in the audience who started screaming; she started swaying back and forth in her chair and exhibited *very* strange behavior. And pretty soon she was just completely hysterical and she fell off her chair and she went unconscious. And everyone—all the meditators there who had been meditating (from—oh, I did 10 to 12 hours a day; some of them did 20 hours a day of meditation) we were all pretty spaced out and we were... just sitting there letting her scream and no one moved to help her. And when I look back on it now, it just really

makes me sick because it reminds me of the crimes being done in New York City where people just stand around and don't move to help. And I'm sure the people were rationalizing this incident in their minds. They probably thought, "She's just exhibiting one of these symptoms of unstressing."

Unstressing, however severe its symptoms, is passed off as a normal concomitant of progress. Shades of Howling Wolf! Vail mentioned that during unstressing the symptoms usually are simply a mild discomfort, with irritability, quick anger and so forth, but she also said, "Some people even have heart attacks—it can get quite severe."

In the case of the disturbed girl at the TM teachers' gathering, Vail said she experienced daily this sensation of "just not caring enough," that seemed to characterize all of those who were deeply involved in TM. She skillfully analyzes the moral side of TM:

I know that when we don't have any kind of a standard, or when we make ourselves the center of the universe—we make ourselves the source of all things—then, really what is to prevent us from justifying anything we do on the basis of, "It's okay?"

On the TM mantra, Vail knew the falsity of Maharishi's public statements. The guru has indicated that the mantra is just a meaningless word, but Vail found that the mantras of many practicing TM, including her own mantra, were the names of various Hindu gods. (see Appendix) She was fully aware of the power of mantra:

The mantra has within its sound structure a formula which will lead a person's conscious mind towards a certain...goal...union with god [Brahman].

Demonic experiences—the encountering of evil spirit beings—is usually passed off as movie material by the average individual (*The Exorcist*, e.g.), but Vail's experiences along these lines were not very entertaining:

After about two years of meditating...I would frequently experience a spirit sitting on either side of me. At first I thought they were my guardian angels....but once I saw one of them and he looked like a demon. (Vail consulted Maharishi himself on this disconcerting experience; the master said that she should just quote her Puja—her initiation ceremony—to the demons and they would leave. She did that and the creatures did leave, but presumably satisfied with Vail's loyalties rather than put off by the *puja.* In any case, they later returned.) Once at a teacher training course in the middle of the night a spirit tried to enter my body because I woke up in the middle of the night and felt the spirit putting pressure all over my head and my body trying to get in.... I commanded it to leave and it went.

Vail's demonic experiences are not at all an isolated case among those practicing TM. The guru is well aware of the phenomenon and passes it off lightly, as Vail relates:

At these teacher training courses a lot of people would get up and talk about their experiences with meditation and their experiences with various spirits, and they'd talk about seeing spirits and experiencing them, and Maharishi would nod and chuckle and say, ''Oh that's quite normal, that's quite to be expected.''

Vail's weird trip also involved her development of psychic powers, such as telepathy, clairvoyance and the early stages of occultic astral projection (spiritual ''traveling''). Her testimony is partially available in the definitive tract *TM— Penetrating the Veil of Deception.*[4]   Unfortunately, although the great dangers of occult/psychic involvement are well documented, many people today continue to play with fire, despite severe consequences.[5]

THE $5,000 TOUR

Greg Randolph, another 5-year meditator and former TM teacher,[6] observed some less-than-spiritual goings-on at the home office, as Maharishi's temper flared one day. It seemed that a Jewish teacher trainee had objected to the obvious idolatry involved with the *puja*; he did not want any part of performing obeisance to the Hindu gods in order to initiate the unsuspecting novices into TM. (Obviously, the teachers see the *puja* for what it really is, and more than a few objections crop up.) Well, the guru really hit the ceiling, according to Randolph; he just "blew up," got very angry and stated that the teacher trainee could either worship the TM tradition or not become a teacher at all.

Becoming a TM teacher can involve the expenditure of up to $5,000, and thus some religious sensitivities get lost along the way.

Close to the inner circles of TM, Greg was able to observe first-hand some of the deceptions involved. He said that TM teachers, who know nearly one hundred percent of the doctrine, are admonished to reveal only one percent to initiates. He reports on the existence of an elite group within the upper levels of the organization consisting of 108 special disciples who gather around Maharishi himself. They get in on all of the super confidential inner workings of the organization, supervise worldwide activities and have the distinct honor of taking care of the guru's personal needs.

There is a plan afoot, according to Greg, to reveal the spiritual nature of TM in the next few years, when presumably enough of the public will be off on some trip or other to accept this sort of spiritualistic dogma more easily. It may also be revealed that there are states to be found beyond even

158

unity consciousness—the ultimate connection to Brahman. Apparently the guru is still evolving; at this point only insiders fully comprehend unity consciousness. The mind boggles at what further states there may be and what they entail.

Greg's description of the intensive teacher training courses makes one think of the adage about the blind leading the blind. It seems that the trainees do a lot of "rounding" (the combination of yoga & TM and may not be able to assimilate the detailed material very efficiently. On top of that, according to Greg, Maharishi is not precisely a gifted lecturer after all; his talks come out a bit on the boring side.

To utilize a human subject in the training course one day, Maharishi came up with an individual who was on his way from the cosmic consciousness state to the unity consciousness state. The fellow was visibly shaken and disconcerted by the experience, very nervous and very scared. The guru placed him in front of the class and explained to him his transitional behavior and its normal discomforts. Maharishi prescribed a special technique to practice, which would alleviate some of the suffering, re-defined the symptoms as beneficial and did manage to make his subject more comfortable (and more devoted than ever to the guru).

The guru's soothing away of what may be warning signs of impending mental trouble is cause for concern. A medical hypnotist does not wish to cover up pain that may well warn of serious illness; a zombie-like patient would be impossible to diagnose. As a principle, depressant drugs, trance states and the like tend to muddle the body and mind's sentinel systems. To alleviate symptoms is not invariably rated as a cure. The severe discomforts of transitional meditators should perhaps be taken much more seriously, and not simply re-defined a beneficial progress.

Greg also explains an insider phenomenon known as "witnessing." Veteran meditators achieve this strange state of paradox where they stand back from life, utterly detached, and merely witness it. Witnesses attain to "the source of all thought. You become so involved with yourself that your concept of what is going on in the world around you becomes very unreal...."

Greg explains the testimony of a witnessing meditator:

> This is what cosmic consciousness is—where you are actually sitting in this vastness, this emptiness of this thing (the world) that has no particular thing you can form a concept about, and looking out at a world around you...and not being able to relate to it. The separateness is at first very scary.

The witness reported the strange sensations of looking at himself doing things—such as driving a car or watching a movie—but not being really in on the thing he was doing. It was as if he were someone else performing for his own observation. "He was not able to feel any relationship to his mother at all," though his family had a normal amount of love in it. He "was very concerned about it (the effects of witnessing) and wondered if he was going to be completely separate from the world around him (permanently). Again he had to be shown more of the Maharishi's teachings where faith comes in."

Greg Randolph was one of those who carried out the re-definition of schizophrenic symptoms as the "higher consciousness" of TM. Rather like Howling Wolf, he helped a confused transcendental meditator get through his frightening experience and denied that his sensations of madness were anything more than the normal rigors of TM progress. In the process he discovered the pathetic "permanent staff members."

> I was on the staff working for my teacher training course and I noticed that there were a few people on the staff who were kind of weird. So I mentioned it to somebody and this person said, 'Oh, they're what is known

as permanent staff members.' What he meant was, these are people who were left over from the teacher training course from the previous year who had been rounding so much they couldn't handle it and were not ready to go back into the world.

One wonders if the permanent staff members will *ever* rejoin us. Meanwhile they have work where their employers are sympathetic. Obviously, no amount of "re-definition" has brought these folks back to where they could be useful, even to TM. Trained as teachers, they remain cached away at headquarters, out of sight of the incoming freshmen, understandably.

Greg endured the ill-named "unstressing" procedure and has a healthy respect now for its potential dangers:

> When your're unstressing for a long time, large a-mounts of this (stress) can come out and actually condition angry moods and cause heart attacks.... Violent, angry rages and all kinds of different unstressings occur. A person could be very violent and angry on one of these courses and somebody who is in cosmic consciousness, who is not able to have that much sympathy or empathy for another person, kind of says, "Now, now," and logically explains that they're unstressing, and the person goes off mad anyway. They do have special techniques for unstressers. They give you acupuncture, massages, warm baths, and so forth. They try to keep you away from drugs if they can.

The unstressing procedure is even carried into supposed past lives, and the bad karma and stress of the past are worked off!

Greg was turned off by the theology of Charles Lutes, SRM president, who said that Jesus was an ordinary man and Christ was the God-reincarnation of him. That is, Jesus

161

of Nazareth was merely a normal man who met a normal death; what we now worship as Christ is the God-realized Jesus. This is a standard occult theme, recurring throughout the teachings of cultic groups, and covered in the Scriptures: "Who is a liar but he that denieth that Jesus is the Christ? He is antichrist that denieth the Father and the Son" (1 Jn. 2:22).

Lutes claims to have encountered Christ in one of his past lives: he was a Roman guard who officiated at Calvary, he says. Like many officers of many other cults, Lutes is able to give first-hand information about the Lord, and such information is typically at variance with the biblical version. With the occult in general, reincarnation illusions are common and some sort of kinship to Jesus is very often claimed. The Lord shares the spotlight with many past sages, but is at least acknowledged as worth mentioning. Since the Biblical doctrines invariably give the lie to cultic worship and practices, Jesus is normally defamed in some way, especially in the denial of His unique divinity.

Greg's report revealed that Lutes broke confidence concerning the highly secret mantras. Questioned by experienced meditators at a TM gathering about the number of existing mantras and their nature, Lutes said the mantras were "favored names of God," and "told them how many there were—fifteen—which most teachers cringe to hear someone say this in public, because a lot of their second lecture (to initiates), which is basically memorized, is on the fact [lie] that there is a mantra for each individual."

So the hocus-pocus about mantras boils down to the fact that there really are very few and that the initiate is duped into simply repeating the name of some Hindu diety over and over in his meditation. No one practicing TM is ever to reveal his mantra, and it now becomes obvious just why— the gods have apparently not selected a mantra for each individual as advertised. Thousands of meditators share a few mantras. A lot of the magic would go out of the mantra-receiving ceremony if the initiates realized they were being given a standardized product rather than a tailor-made original for their own personal use.

Greg was bothered by this revelation, as were a great many of the sincere TM teachers. The teachers are saddled with the task of promoting the exclusivity of the mantras and the lie is so obvious.

Greg was also disturbed by several bad trips he encountered among the meditators. An epileptic whose seizures were supposed to abate with TM actually experienced more severe seizures. A case of overwhelming self-withdrawal troubled Greg. He himself suffered something like a heart attack while under TM—fifteen to twenty minutes of extreme chest pain, which left him reeling. He also experienced blackouts for up to twenty hours per day for a two-week period. The cosmic consciousness experience of a TM friend who "had a seizure of some kind and found he didn't have control over his body for a whole evening" also alarmed him. This individual had an upsetting demonic experience in which he was being perceived by two demons as if he were on display in a zoo.

Greg was more disturbed, however, by the simple lack of veracity of the movement. "One of the things about teaching TM that was always hard to swallow was out-and-out lying to people."

Greg's testimony was examined by a clinical psychologist, who evaluated it:

> The process described by Mr. Randolph [unstressing] can lead to a tremendous amount of stress on the individual. Some people can bear up under this kind of stress and some people will crack. It's a very stressful thing . . . you can *really* lose touch. In dealing with altered states of awareness, all sorts of bizarre things can happen.

She also felt that the TM process tended to break down and confuse the natural conscious barrier separating reality from unreality.

163

TAKE ONLY AS DIRECTED

Joan Wheeler was less dedicated to TM than many, meditating inconsistently for 2 years, but qualifying to teach the Science of Creative Intelligence on the high school level. 7 She was not qualified to dispense mantras. She mainly practiced TM because of the physical relaxation involved, and says that over her two-year period "the meditation was generally pleasurable, although it did not fulfill my spiritual needs." She noticed that some people were motivated to try to hurry through training courses, although Maharishi counseled against this:

> There are negative effects of meditation—people can get extremely up-tight and argumentative. This occurs because people meditate longer than they are told to in an attempt to get somewhere faster. This was especially noticeable at long courses such as SCI training. Although Maharishi requested that no one do long periods of rounding, his request was not always honored.

Apparently the doctor had discovered the potency of his medicine. The guru instructed his disciples on how to handle the programs—but rather like those of the drug culture, who perennially search for a greater "high," some had over-dosed.

This is one great failing of TM—it has but one instructor who ultimately dispenses all of its dogma. Maharishi has many functionaries, as we have seen, but remains the sole repository of doctrinal knowledge. We noted that few meditators really study the guru's written works, and drop-out testimony attests to a fact many would suspect, that the followers rush through the steps of their discipline, perhaps emerging really unprepared to handle for themselves, much less dispense to others, such potent stuff. The fact that meditators are qualified by the movement to teach

TM to high school students after only two years or less of meditating suggests that many amateurs are on the loose with this personality-altering program. The TM teacher training programs is only three months long. Ex-teachers have even mentioned that husbands and wives are separated into different rooms during the process of rounding because of the potential conflicts that occur during unstressing.

TUNED IN AND TURNED OFF

John Vos was once the consummate TMer.[8] He was initiated right at the beginning of the American thrust of the movement in 1968 by Jerry Jarvis, the National Director of SIMS-IMS, and he gladly participated in the original Keith Wallace TM physiology experiments as part of his doctoral studies at the UCLA Medical School.[9]

He studied hard, was very actively involved in the movement, and applied himself arduously to the most advanced coursework and techniques. He studied Maharishi's tapes, films and writings and he became a truly knowledgeable and dedicated disciple.

Now he's completely turned off.

He wasn't able to put up with the description of TM as purely scientific. ''I knew that to be false, and anyone who has practiced TM any length of time and is honest knows this.'' He became downright scared at the pretensions of the movement, such as the Jarvis statement, ''There should be *a law* that everyone should have to practice TM so they wouldn't be throwing their tension out into society.''

John was on the scene when Maharishi used to call a spade a spade. In those days the guru always spoke of TM as completely religious and not scientific in nature. His present marketing technique had not yet occurred to him, and the representations were more honest. The utter deceptions that began to occur when Maharishi learned how to peddle his program as scientific disgusted John, and the extravagant claims for TM made him cynical.

165

John also saw first-hand some of the more bizarre effects of advanced TM, including the unstressing case of a friend who "became so angry and furious and went into such a rage that he smashed all the furniture in his apartment and the pictures on the walls." John emphasizes that similar unstressing incidents are not uncommon:

> I rarely met a meditator that didn't speak of various incredible unstressing experiences they had gone through over periods of several minutes or longer— *sometimes several weeks.* It's very much of a universal thing among meditators and it comes in various degrees of intensity. I have seen a lot of unstressing while I was a meditator and it's not uncommon for meditators to become extremely violent, to break things, to go into uncontrollable fits of rage, even to assault people. It's not uncommon at all. In fact, Maharishi kept shortening the amount of TM because the unstressing people were going through was just completely uncontrollable.

Unstressing, the boot camp for higher consciousness, has been troublesome for the guru right along, and, as John points out, he has been forced to lower his dosages. It certainly looks bad for a program called "transcendental," involving something so peaceful-sounding as "meditation," to breed such outbursts of rage and violence. One cannot help wondering at the guru's claim that TM will result in the cessation of all wars and at last bring global peace. A whole city of folks undergoing unstressing presents a picture too frightening to look at, not to mention the whole world.

But the guru has found another solution, besides simply advising his followers to take less of his cure. This one is a masterpiece for the PR-minded Maharishi. This solution takes care of all sorts of loose ends.

He has recently changed the term "unstressing" to "normalization."

Now everybody can relax.

The most discouraging case for John was the commitment of a meditator to the Camarillo State Mental Hospital in California for a period of six months. The meditator simply broke under the strain of his radical and unmanageable personality change, and while true mental illness is more the exception than the rule in TM, John was disgusted. Two attending psychiatrists insisted on the cessation of TM in this case, having determined no other psychological history in the patient that could have caused such a complete breakdown. The TM was held totally responsible in this particular instance and its stoppage was a necessary part of the treatment.

John verified for himself that TM was harmful and he ultimately gave up the program.

ALL IN THE FAMILY

Yvonne Maher was so sold on TM that she had her children initiated, down to her eight year old.[10] But after two years of deeply disturbing occult experiences she gave it all up. She was studying to become an instructor at the time she dropped out in confusion and fear.

"During my meditation I had experiences of precognition (visions of the future), astral projection and the sensation of the presence of nebulous forms around me. I also experienced TM unstressing which produced a lot of anger and rage inside of me. Some of my TM friends also had that experience but we were cautioned never to discuss this with anyone but our instructor.

"About a month after I stopped meditating I experienced the terribly frightening presence of some kind of demonic being in my room. The room had seemed to grow colder and colder, and twice I got up to turn up the heat, to no avail. Suddenly the room seemed icy cold and I became aware of this 'presence.' I could not see a definite form, but I could sense when the thing changed direction as it moved about. I could feel energy coming from the thing, but I felt it as extreme coldness. I tried to continue to read but the ink started to run down the pages before my eyes. I felt trapped and very afraid.

"This demon, and I do feel the thing was a demon, did not leave my room until almost daybreak, as I sat paralyzed with fear.

"That wasn't my first weird experience associated with TM. I also had on occasion experienced some kind of 'spirit' sitting in the back seat of my car as I drove. A close friend of mine, who was no artist, produced a very good painting of Maharishi while under the influence of some unexplainable inspiration she was experiencing." The phenomenon of 'automatic writing' is quite common in occult circles; the writer, or typer, writes out some kind of dogma dictated by the spirit being experienced. Typically the writing is quite different from the normal vernacular of the writer. Many occult leaders claim to get their information from their spirit-world contacts in this way, even from extra-terrestrial beings. (See the authors' *UFOs . . . What On Earth Is Happening?*.) We assume that artistic-minded spirits also provide painting skills when the occasion calls.

Mrs. Maher also suffered psychological damage from her TM experience and its occult concomitants. "It took several months of very difficult therapy to overcome these problems. I definitely do not recommend TM to anyone. I know of other people who were harmed by it.

"My youngest child was given a 'walking mantra,' with which she meditated while being engaged in other activities. She was not given a regular mantra, I was told, because she might go so far under that she would never come out. Another daughter, using a standard mantra, would come out of her particular meditation too quickly sobbing uncontrollably, almost hysterically, and it distressed me.

"There were times when my TM produced an apathy in

me, and in my TM friends, to the extent that we really lost all ambition and energy to do the simplest tasks.''

"A MORE EXCELLENT WAY"

It should be stressed that these are not such special cases. The authors could probably make a whole book of similar devastating testimonies about the rigors of TM, the quiet way to inner peace. The individuals who offered their experiences here were not paid for them and were found merely among the acquaintances of co-author John Weldon. Anyone questioning TM devotees would likely come up with similar reports about the program, assuming a willingness to give honest answers.

Of course, satisfied customers are also to be found. Some people are fascinated with the supernatural, and with world-changing movements in general. It is presently fashionable to try to change the world, and we can sympathize, the world being what it is.

But we think that the fascination with supernatural things and with God-realization, increasingly apparent today, comes from an honest hunger common to all men. We *do* want to find God today, and we all need to find him. There is little doubt that the world in general is headed in the wrong direction and thinking people are looking for alternatives.

Knowing God personally, we think, is a viable alternative to a purely materialistic life, but we advocate the true God. We think that the God of the Bible is the answer to all human needs, and we think He is still very much in charge and very much aware of what troubles we have. We think He is waiting patiently for people to come to Him as He always has. And we think He compares very well to such difficult and dangerous systems as TM.

In our final chapter we want to compare the true God against this manufactured alternative. The authors are believing Christians whose life experiences, including meditation of the Biblical kind and of supernatural activity originating with the true God, provide a sharp contrast to the religion of transcendental meditation.

FOOTNOTES: CHAPTER SEVEN

Introductory quotations: *Philosophy of Meditation*, p. 54; *Meditations*, p. 51; *Psychology Today*, Dec. 1975, p. 4; *On the Bhagavad Gita*, p. 364; Zaehner, *Zen*, *Drugs*, *Mysticism*, pp. 108-9; *On the Bhagavad Gita*, p. 340; Record Album.

1. Taped interview with Chuck Simmons of CARIS, P.O. Box 265, Whittier, CA 90608, published partially in *TM, Penetrating the Veil of Deception*, P.O. Box 4308, Berkeley, CA

2. Shah, *The Meditators*, p. 117.

3. Taped interview with Chuck Simmons and all her statements hereafter unless noted otherwise.

4. Spiritual Counterfeits Project, P.O. Box 4308, Berkeley, CA.

5. Kurt Koch, *Between Christ and Satan, Christian Counseling and Occultism, Occult Bondage and Deliverance* (Kregel); Montgomery, ed., *Demon Possession* (Bethany, 1976); Martin Ebon, *The Satan Trap: Dangers of the Occult* (Doubleday, 1976), etc.

6. Taped interview conducted by Dave Haddon, SCP, and all of his statements hereafter.

7. Personal interview conducted by the author, Jan. 1976.

8. Personal interview conducted by the author, Jan. 1976.

9. Forem, p. 46-7. The experiments were done at the TM center, not UCLA.

10. Personal interview conducted by the author, Feb. 1976.

"If we belong to Christianity, the scriptures of Christianity tell us what is right and wrong.... It is better to follow the scriptures of one's own religion."

Maharishi

"The mystic who triumphantly realizes his essential oneness with God, or the World-Order, or the Divine, knowing himself in serene equanimity the supreme master of the universe and of his own destiny, and who by marvelous feats of moral self-restraint offers a fascinating example of splendid humanity...nevertheless, in the light of Biblical revelation, commits in this sublime way the root sin of mankind— 'to be like God.' In other words: *he repeats the Fall*"

Hendrik Kraemer

"If God and the human soul were completely different, no amount of logical reasoning or meditation could lead us to the reality of God."

Radhakrishnan

"The worm that crawls under our feet is the brother of the Nazarene."

Swami Viveananda

"No man, no Christian should ever suffer,..."

Maharishi

"The man of character is usually the man who has suffered; the life that is free from suffering is often the life that is empty or shallow or superficial or unsympathetic. Suffering and tragedy introduce into life a dimension which nothing else can. The righteous do suffer, the most righteous man who ever lived, the perfect man, suffered more than any other; and in the words of the author of Hebrews, 'He became complete through the things which He suffered.' "

Author unknown

"For to you it has been granted for Christ's sake, not only to believe in Him, but also to suffer for His sake."

Philippians 1:29

CHAPTER EIGHT

MAHARISHI OR JESUS:
WHICH WAY TO GOD?

One part of the TM non-religion pitch is that the stuff never can conflict with anybody's religion. In fact, according to the publicity, it helps one appreciate one's own religion better.

As we have seen, however, TM is a religion, and one whose claims style it to replace all other religions. If it is to usher in a New Age of Enlightenment, we hardly need the Christian Kingdom of the future, or the Jewish Messianic Age or even the communistic utopia so long in transit. If we are to have world peace, personal happiness and all the other of Maharishi's panaceas, we're wasting our time trying to contact God in heaven, so reluctant to bring us what the guru offers so cheaply.

Maharishi does hedge a bit on what TM may do to one's religious concepts, asserting that, "One will find that basically the truth of one's own religion is the basic truth of the religions of others," and that finally, all religion boils down to the Hindu God-realization. [1] If we fail to perceive this we are ignorant. There is little room left for any other religion when TM is present since TM is the only successful path to God-realization for non-Hindus and the best path for Hindus. [2] The guru thinks that "the realization of the state of all knowledge [TM] is the only way to salvation and success in life; there is no other way.[3]" He says, in contradiction to Jesus (John 14:6) that without "Union brought about through Transcendental Meditation...there is no way out.[4]"

In this last chapter we want to compare TM with Christianity, the world's dominant religion. There are some parallels apparent, and Bible-believing Christians have expected that when the false prophets announced by the Lord would come, they would be clever counterfeiters.

TM AND CM

American culture is basically a Christian culture, or perhaps a post-Christian culture. While there are not a great many true Christians making the headlines today, and although the last finished Christian ascended to His Father long ago, this country is still, as founded, a Christian culture.

The guru realizes that. He said, "I am a priest and I love Christianity and religion. [5]" (One is somewhat heartened to note his distinction between Christianity and "religion." Has the guru the insight to see that all religions involve working one's way to God on the basis of personal merit while Christianity is soundly based on grace—merely accepting the *free gift* of salvation on the merit of Jesus Christ?)

Many American clergymen, however, Jewish, Catholic and Protestant, have joined the purveyors of TM in calling it compatible with American religious beliefs in general, and even complimentary to Christianity. [6] We want to examine that.

CM, or Christian meditation, if we may coin a term, is a valid part of the Christian experience, but is greatly different than Maharishi's meditation.[7] CM is practical, not mystical; aimed at activity, not a passive void. The Christian contemplates and communicates with God; the TMer cultivates an absence of communication and tries to ''experience'' an undefinable Being (Brahman).

CM reaches actively toward a personal, loving God; TM centers passively on an impersonal elusive ''It.'' In CM one ponders and applies God's Word and His revealed character; the idea is to accomplish practical spiritual endeavors with the aid of a caring God. In TM one retreats from practicalities and contemplates nothing but the mantra—undefined even for the meditator; the idea is to avoid all endeavors of any sort leaving all action up to Brahman (when It is located).

CM is aimed at mental contentment, and the peace it produces is rational. TM is aimed at blanking out, and the bliss it produces is irrational. CM looks to God's standards with a view to growing closer to them. TM seeks to merge with its god, so that the meditator becomes god. The Christian is a creation of God. The TMer becomes the creator himself, he supposes.

The very activity in the two kinds of meditation differs fundamentally. To begin with, Christian meditation is not an end in itself; Christian action is the point of CM. For the TMer, the meditation is his sole activity, and it alone is to make him into God. There is no other activity in TM apart from the repetition of the mantra; it is supposed to take care of all progress and all other activity by itself.

Interestingly, Jesus warned against this kind of repetitive incantation, and drew a distinction between it and true prayer:

> But when ye pray, use not vain repetitions as the heathen do; for they think that they shall be heard for

their much speaking. Be not therefore like unto them: for your father knoweth what things ye have need of, before ye ask him. (Matt. 6:7-8)

God's attributes, as given in the Scriptures, are mercy, love, justice, etc., and the CMer contemplates those knowledgeably. The attributes of Brahman are purposefully unknown. Other people, all creations of God, are deeply respected in CM. TM considers them illusory. The Christian seeks to love all men, in accordance with his example in Christ. The TMer can be indifferent to other human beings, in accordance with his example in Brahman. There is no *basis* for concern among men.

TM has caught on well in the U.S. because of the present spiritual starvation. People are reaching out for something mystical, so disconcerted are they with the decline of the material way of life around them. Young people especially become fascinated with the charisma of "mysticism" associated with eastern concepts of religion, which contrasts so strongly with the highly pragmatic, materialistic western way of thinking. They often do not appreciate that the Bible is a very mystical book, and one to compete with the subtlest of Hindu writ. The big difference is, of course, that at its most mystical point, the Bible still draws the clear distinction between man and God. Ezekiel, Daniel, John in Revelation; all are seen in contrast to their Revealer, to the One who provides their visions and prophecies. In the eastern mysticism one eventually *becomes* God, and the vital distinction between Creator and creature is lost. This is detrimental to the creature, to say the least.

The greater distinction is of course that the Bible is a true and reliable book, with fulfilled prophecies, accurate assessments of the human condition, salvation that delivers and much *evidence* in its favor.[8] The Bible can be tried and not found lacking; the eastern mysticism has definitely not stood up to scrutiny.

TM and CM are polar opposites, though the guru has borrowed some handy and trusted religious doctrine. It's of no matter, though, whether one wears the cosmetics of an eastern mystic to impress God. "As a man thinketh in his heart so is he," God has said. (Prov. 23:7) TM leads you to think you're Brahman with the result that you become Brahman.[9]

TM qualifies, in the light of CM, as idolatry: The worship of some man-made god is an old story, as we have said, and the only different feature of TM is in its superficial appeal to "modern" thinking. One should be concerned with Psalm 19:14:

> "Let the words of my mouth and the meditation of my heart be acceptable in Thy sight, O Lord, my rock and my redeemer."

GOD VS. BRAHMAN

Brahman is one hard god to get to know, as we have illustrated. He, or "It," is totally impersonal, indefinable, unmanifested, etc., so that logically we can say nothing about Brahman.[10] But Maharishi has described Brahman, whom he presumably knows, or is, although his description leaves one hungry again.

The guru says that Brahman is without quality, feature or attribute, impersonal, formless and indescribable.[11] It (Brahman) is unmanifested and forever the same, but also It is the entire creation, but only in the sense of an illusion. This is It's *lila*, or game-playing.[12] Maharishi's ultimate riddle about Brahman may be:

> The Absolute is said to be almighty, but not in the sense that It is able to do everything. This is because being everything, It cannot do anything and cannot know anything. It is beyond doing and knowing.[13]

Compared to that helpful definition, the God of Abraham, Isaac, and Jacob becomes a masterstroke of clarity and simplicity. And He is, of course, further manifested to the world as Jesus Christ, so that His attributes both in heaven and earth are plainly presented.[14] Finally, His present manifestation as the Holy Spirit is available to all, and should satisfy the fascination with mysticism of those inclined toward the eastern religions. The Biblical God, expressed as the trinity, does not operate in secrecy or illusion. He *is* almighty, and acts as such throughout creation. He has the prime attribute, where men are concerned, of loving and wishing to be loved in return.

His attitude is very clear, and hardly the evasive attitude of the inexplicable Brahman: "I stand at the door and knock," He says. "Ask and it shall be given...seek and ye shall find." For those seeking a god, the Original is a breath of fresh air. He can be loved, worshipped, enjoyed, known personally, and meditated upon. He is distinct from His creation so that we don't end up "becoming God" and worshipping ourselves.[15]

Worship of the Biblical God involves a much better future than the pursuit of Brahman. Bible prophecy tells of the coming Kingdom on earth, and ultimately eternity, where true bliss will reign endlessly. With Brahman, however, there will be a universal dissolution at the end of the ages and only Brahman himself will be left.[16] It plays with human history for a time, sporting with Its *lila*, and then draws creation back into Itself.[17]

With God, all human acts count. We are His children, He has said, at least those of us who choose to be. But in Brahman's scheme of things no segment of history, no personal act, no human existence ultimately has any meaning whatever; Brahman is the only reality and only Brahman exists, whether we believe in him or not. It is incapable of love and couldn't care less about the whole subject.

But God cares. The Bible is the story of God's deep

concern for His children and His provision for them. Brahman, on the other hand, is the picture of indifference, even mischief, toward mankind. Brahman's serene unconcern with the world stands in sharp contrast to the sacrifice of Jesus Christ for the redemption of the human race; God acts, while Brahman plays.

Finally, there is this matter of good and evil, said not to exist in Brahman's system. Few men anywhere subscribe to this at heart, though dogma can sway human minds. In TM, Brahman is the author of evil and makes no distinction between good and evil.[18] In the Bible God created only good; a good world, a good man and a good woman.[19] The man and woman were created with free wills, not as puppets, and they, not God, were the authors of evil. Satan is given in the Bible as the original source of evil, and God the original source of good, so that there is certainly a contrast between the two.

As with the comparison of TM and CM, Brahman and God are utter opposites.

SIN AND ITS ANTIDOTE

TM and Christianity vastly differ on the matters of sin and salvation. The central message of the Bible is that man is separated from God by his sins and that the sacrifice of Jesus Christ reconciles man to God. God says "But your iniquities have made a separation between you and your God." (Isa. 59:2) However, Christ accepted the penalty for all men's sins, and all men believing in Christ are spared this penalty. In TM, sin is just a matter of ignorance—the failure of a man to realize that he is God.[20] There is no sense of a violation in the TM concept of sin. The TM god has no holy character to be violated; in fact, no character whatsoever. Salvation in TM is gained by God-realization—conquering one's ignorance and finding one's own diety within,[21] i.e. by realizing there is no separation from God.

In Christianity men come to God by realizing there *is* a separation between them and that Christ alone bridges that chasm. In TM there is no difference between men and God, so neither forgiveness nor reconciliation are needed. Maharishi says, "Thus it is clear that the realization of the Impersonal is merely arriving at one's own Being. And this shows that there exists no 'path' between the experiencer and the Impersonal.[22]" Jesus said, "I am the way, the truth, and the life. No man comes to the Father but by me." (John 14:6)

The logic of Christianity is that Christ, though sinless, willingly suffered what would rightfully be the penalty of each sinful man and thus died for all men. It is not that Christians are without sin; their sins have been paid for. God must be just. He must judge sin: The sacrifice of the perfectly sinless Christ fulfills the obligation. Men need only believe this in order to be forgiven.

Maharishi questions this doctrine and even the suffering of Christ:

> I don't think Christ ever suffered or Christ could suffer...it is a pity that Christ is talked of in terms of suffering...those who count upon the suffering [for salvation, have] a wrong interpretation of the life of Christ and the message of Christ. It is wrong.[23]"

In the world of Maharishi there is no suffering of course, particularly for so obviously a "God-realized" individual as Jesus Christ. Jesus of all people would have been the first to know that "Man is born of bliss," and "Life is bliss," in words of the guru.[24] Surely Christ did not suffer, and surely He did not dream that men needed His death as a propitiation for their sins, thinks Maharishi.

But Jesus Himself testified otherwise:

> O foolish men and slow of heart to believe in all that the prophets have spoken! Was it not necessary for the Messiah to suffer these things, and to enter into this glory? (Luke 24:25)

We have a biblical picture of Jesus contemplating His impending crucifixion. We certainly don't get the idea of bliss in His anxiety. We see Him suffering:

> And being in an agony he prayed more earnestly; and his sweat was, as it were, great drops of blood falling to the ground (Luke 22:24).

All Scripture, including Old Testament prophecy (Isa. 53, etc.) hails the very suffering of the Messiah as a necessary substitutionary sacrifice, and His resurrection as the sign of true salvation:

> Thus it is written, that the Christ should suffer and rise again from the dead the third day. (Luke 24:46) And He Himself bore our sins in His body on the cross, that we might die to sin and live to righteousness, for by His wounds you were healed. (Pet. 2:24)

Confronting Maharishi in his own field is difficult for many, requiring scientific data and some knowledge of Hindu practices to pick through his argot. But when he takes on the Scriptures and comments on the motives of Christ he reveals a lack of spiritual grasp, or at least a disrespect for the Bible. To reduce the Savior to terms of TM categories is rather defensive, if not utterly blasphemous, and to analyze the work of Christ as being other than the gospel says it is, is merely a characteristic of false prophets in general.

The Bible is, of course, the best source of information we have about Jesus Christ, though many men have said and written many philosophies in their wrestlings with the simplicity of God's Word. The guru's dismissal of Christian salvation in favor of the TM self-diety concept is spiritually immature, and dangerous to impressionable people.

Apart from the disagreements over the efficacy of Christ's sacrifice for salvation, TM and Christianity differ on every basic doctrine[25] including what ultimately happens to the individual who is completely consecrated. Being ''saved'' in TM is quite a different thing than being saved in Christianity.

The TM devotee gets more or less swallowed up into Brahman and ultimately becomes non-existent forever. With reincarnation philosophies in general, individuality is pointless; the personality that we now are will change and change again, and ultimately be totally eliminated. With Christ's salvation, the individual that we now are is the one saved; we go as we are, and what we are is what He gets. The Christian is conscious of being redeemed and reconciled to God as he is. The TMer loses all personal identity and becomes something other than what he is, as he lives, and he finally comes to nothing, literally.

DEATH

Death is not very important to those holding the Hinduistic views, as we saw in the case of Charles Manson. Death is a transitional stage in TM and nothing to be concerned about.

Death to the Christian is also not to be feared, as the Christian has been granted eternal life and goes to be with God, according to the Scriptures. Death of the body comes to every mortal man, but the Christian is relieved of the fear of death of the soul. (Cor. 15:22-23)

While he lives, the Christian has an entirely different feeling about death than the TMer does. For the Christian death marks the end of his earthly service for the Lord. For the TMer death makes no difference in his relationship to Brahman.

182

In Maharishi's view, the body and personality are not the real individual. When a TMer dies, "He remains what he was—Brahman—but without the individual body.[26]" The experience of the higher TM states, rather like the LSD and mediumistic experiences, takes away the natural fear of death built into each of us.[27] We have already noted the casual official attitude toward death in the TM movement: the TMer would encounter Guru Dev, be given a new mantra, and continue to conduct business as usual. There was no reason to fear this transition, and no concern over suicides among the TM teachers.

This is an unnatural attitude in the Christian view. Every human being since the Garden of Eden has a God-made fear of death because, spiritually speaking, God hates death.[28] Death was the punishment meted out for sin by a reluctant God to Adam and Eve, who were originally made immortal. "The wages of sin is death," the Bible says, and that's all death is. Wherever there is sin, there is death. Death comes to every man because of his sins, in the Christian view.

But death can be defeated, as it was by Jesus, who was without sin.

God does not favor death ("He does not desire even one to perish"), but wishes for every human being to defeat it. We can—every one of us—by participating in the vicarious sacrifice of Christ. There is no guarantee, in all of Hinduism, that a given individual will survive death. The coming of a new incarnation, if it does indeed come, is hardly comforting. But the Bible guarantees this most incredible of promises, that the Christian will go on alive and perfected as the individual he is, just as Jesus came back from death as the individual He was. However we must believe in Christ for this salvation, and not in ourselves, as in TM. The real question is this: "Does man contain within himself all that can be required of him for time and eternity? TM says yes, "Inner man is divine, Brahman, and self-sufficient." God says, "Behold, I will enter into judgement with you, because you say, 'I have not sinned.' '' (Jeremiah 2:35)

It is the built-in fear of death that makes each of us realize somewhere within us that there will be an accounting of our behavior after death. As God judged His original children in the Garden, so He will judge each of us. But Christians will be seen ''in the robes of righteousness of Jesus Christ,'' the Scriptures say. That is, Christ has already paid for the sins of those who follow Him and they will *not* be punished. ''I am come that they might have life,'' He said (Jn. 10:10), ''and have it more abundantly.''

Now it is that initial fear of death—that inner knowledge that each individual's behavior *is* important to the Creator—that persuades men to consider Christ. If there is a way out of that judgement, sensible men will take it, and that is, in its simplest form, God's provision for the redemption of men.

Remove that fear of death, as TM does, and somehow there results an indifference toward good and evil. Behavior is no longer important. Brahman doesn't care one way or the other about the TMer's behavior.

Obviously, the knowledgeable TMer feels he has no need of redemption and no need of God's plan for it.

Since he has sins, he will die. God will be obliged to judge him, and without his participation in God's plan for redemption he will not gain eternal life.

LIFE

With all due respect for the profundities of Maharishi's system, and the thinking of all the previous Hindu sages, we still think God's remedy is the best.

The Christian life before and after death is better. It's God's way, in agreement with the Creator and all of His creation. It requires no special dogma, no repeating of formulas, no tying up with a PR movement, no lying to new converts, no debilitating effects on the mind and body, no

184

risk of schizophrenia or suicide, no violence, no rages, no indifference toward life, no indifference toward death.

It *will* bring world peace and it *does* make people feel better, all day every day, not in just two sessions a day of blanking out. It is useful, industrious behavior, aimed at loving and helping all men. It opposes poverty and paganism, which seem to travel hand in hand in the world, and it is tried and true—far and away the world's most popular, effective and accurate way of encountering God.

Interestingly, all of the dissatisfied TM customers we quoted in the previous chapter are today committed Christians. Despite their long allegiance to TM and their considerable experience with the program, they all found what they were looking for in Jesus Christ.

Christianity is an open book—the Bible—available to all, except where it is suppressed by atheists who fear its power to change men. The book is logical, easily understood in modern translations, if not in the celebrated and widely quoted King James version, and taught far and wide. People differ about minor points within the Scriptures but all agree on the message of salvation—that Christ died for our sins.

Coming to Christ and gaining salvation is simple—infinitly simpler than transcendental meditation or any other of the cultic solutions to the human condition. The Bible says that God has made it simple because He wants men to live, not die.

To become a Christian one need only believe in Christ. Believe that His sacrifice does in fact pay for all your sins, past, present and future, and you are saved.

Of course, to believe in Christ one must get to know Him. He is fully introduced in the Bible, in the churches who honor Him and by all believing Christians. Christ is much more available than TM and no fee is necessary. Every reader must know a true Christian; Christ actually resides in that person. The Christian can make Christ known to you.

185

Christians generally hold that a given moment of conversion is a good idea—a time when you say to the Lord, "Come into my life, forgive my sins, I believe." This is biblical. People "received" Christ when He came. (Jn. 1:12; Jn. 12:12) Believing Christians (we say "believing" Christians because the term Christian has been abused many times by unbelievers) tend to remember the day of their conversion—their re-birthday, as it were. (Jn. 3:3)

Come to Christ and enjoy not only a better, more abundant life now, but real joy to come. Participate with us in the Kingdom to come where there will be at last "Peace on earth, good will toward men," and where God's will "will be done on earth as it is in heaven."

Biblical prophecy, if not the various false prophets and cults, indicates that there is to be something of a great change in human affairs shortly. God's harvest of men is to cease at the end of this church age, and that end may be near. "This is the hour," the Bible says, to gain assurance of a place in God's Kingdom to come.

If you delay your salvation you do take a certain chance on world affairs, the possibility of your own death and the timing of God's plans. But some people need time to think. While you're thinking, think about God, not some side issue like TM or one of the other "deliverance" cults around these days. We have a clever enemy—not Maharishi, but God's original enemy—who seeks always to turn men from salvation. He tries various things which appeal to various men; some like quasi-religious cults, some like strange things such as seances and UFO's, and all alike sin, which distracts men from God. When thinking about a serious matter like the big question of who you really are and where you're going eventually, think rationally and gather evidence. We naturally recommend the Bible, the Christians and the churches, where God is easily found, but the apostle Paul pointed out that God can be clearly seen in nature itself. Look around you. Decide whether a loving creative God made all this, or whether it was made by Brahman, or happened by accident.

The authors are believing Christians. We don't condone TM. We would be poor Christians if we didn't love all men. We have assembled evidence against a false religion for the use of men who need a real one. Frankly, there was not room in this book to print all the evidence we mustered, and we stand rather amazed at this point at the mischief we've uncovered in this research. Maharishi and his friends are really up to something very unwise, and we don't want to see it happen to people. If you are practicing TM, we hope you will re-consider.

> Don't fall into the TM trap. Go with Jesus instead. He said, "Follow Me."

You can receive Christ right now simply by saying the following prayer: "Thank you, Jesus Christ, for dying for my sins. I receive you right now as my Savior and Lord and ask you to come into my life and make me the kind of person you want me to be." Right now why don't you put this book aside and come to know Jesus Christ personally? Your entire life can be radically transformed to the kind of life you want it to be. Fulfilled, joyous, challenging and creative. You have everything to gain or everything to lose by this one decision. It's up to you.

If you just received Jesus Christ we want to be the first to congratulate you. Your new life is just beginning, and we couldn't be happier. The joy and fulfillment of your new life in Christ will increase steadily. All your sins are now forgiven and you are God's own child. (I John 3:1) You can be certain that you now have eternal life. (I John 5:13) God has said "I will never desert you. Nor will I ever forsake you." (Hebrews 13:5) Now that you are a new person in Christ Jesus, the best way to grow as a Christian is to read the Bible. A good place to start is the Gospel of John. Ask Christ to teach you as you read and He will. Seeking out other true believers in Christ and fellowshipping with them will also be helpful. One of the best books we know of to get you on a solid footing spiritually is Hal Lindseys *THE LIBERATION OF PLANET EARTH.* We recommend it highly. Hallelujah!

FOOTNOTES: CHAPTER EIGHT

Introductory quotations: *Transcendental Meditation*, p. 131; *Religion and Christian Faith* (London; Lutterworth, 1956), p. 335, from Zaehner, p. 85; Gopi Krishna, *The Awakening of Kundalini*, p. 70; Swami Prabhavananda, *Yoga and Mysticism* (Vedanta, 1972), p. 10; *Meditations*, p. 63; Source unknown; The Bible.

1. Maharishi, *Transcendental Meditation*, pp. 220-221, 235, 254.

2. *Ibid.*, pp. 249-55, 265-94; *Meditations of Maharishi*, pp. 187-8, *On the Bhagavad Gita*, p. 229.

3. Maharishi, *On the Bhagavad Gita*, pp. 228-9.

4. *Ibid.*, p. 299.

5. Fairfield (Iowa) *Ledger*, Oct. 3, 1975.

6. See *The TM Book.*

7. For Biblical references to meditation and chapter documentation on CM see Joshua 1:8, Psalm 1:2, 3; 4:4; 49:3; 77:10-12; 119; 143:5; Philippians 4:8.

8. See J. McDowell, *Evidence That Demands a Verdict*, Vol. I; H. Morris, *Many Infallible Proofs;* F. Schaeffer, *He Is There and He Is Not Silent*, especially.

9. Mundaka Upanishad III. ii.9.

10. *On the Bhagavad Gita*, pp. 440-1.

11. *Transcendental Meditation*, pp. 124, 265-6.

12. See Note 17.

13. *Transcendental Meditation*, p. 267, and *Love and God*.

14. Hebrews 1:1-3; Col. 2:9.

15. *Transcendental Meditation*, p. 268.

16. *Ibid.*, pp. 28, 269-72; *On the Bhagavad Gita*, pp. 261; *Meditations of Maharishi*, pp. 14-15.

17. *On the Bhagavad Gita*, pp. 250, 261, 416, 491-2; *Transcendental Meditation*, pp. 28-36, 276.

18. *Meditations*, p. 141; *Transcendental Meditation*, p. 295; *On the Bhagavad Gita*, pp. 130, 175, 203, 219; *Kaushitaki Upanishad* 3:1-2, 8; *Taittirya Upanishad* II.9.

19. Genesis 1:31.

20. *Transcendental Meditation*, p. 206; *On the Bhagavad Gita*, pp. 78, 110, 274, 237-40; *Meditations*, pp. 31, 78-9, 57, 155.

21. *Meditations of Maharishi*, pp. 176-7.

22. *Transcendental Meditation*, p. 268.

23. *Meditations*, p. 124.

24. *Ibid.*, pp. 154-6.

25. *Transcendental Meditation*, pp. 73, 248-9, 212; *On the Bhagavad Gita*, pp. 187, 263, 265, 373, 202-3, 395, 312, 339; *Meditations*, pp. 19, 64-6, 169, 70, 63, 123-4, 178, 155, 162, etc. In TM, Christianity is the greatest of evils: *Transcendental Meditation*, pp. 249-55, 204, 247-8; *Gita*, pp. 52, 233, 283-7, 379, 202; *Meditations*, pp. 33, 61-3, 89, 107-9, 123-7, 157-8.

26. *On the Bhagavad Gita*, p. 292.

27. LeShan, p. 133; Gopi Krishna, *The Awakening of Kundalini* (Dutton, 1975), pp. 73-4; Whie, ed., *The Highest State of Consciousness*, pp. 304, 465; Campbell, p. 168; Rieker, p. 86, 112.

28. I Corinthians 15:26, 55-57.

APPENDIX ONE:
TM MANTRAS AND HINDU GODS

The *Classical Dictionary of India* says, "Mantras are used in the performance of every religious rite.[1]" TM mantras are not "meaningless sounds," as Maharishi and TM proponents proclaim.

The following is a principal list of TM *mantras* (literally, mind-control) verified as accurate by two ex-teachers, Gregg Randolph and Vail Hamilton. They are assigned by age: 0-11 years for the first, two-year segments thereafter for the next seven, one four-year segment, five-year segments for the subsequent six mantras, and the final one for age sixty and over: eng, em, enga, ema, ieng, ienga, iema, shirim, shiring, kirim, kiring, hirim, hiring, sham, shama. I have come across others in my research and these include: a-em, ram, hum, hrim, Krim, ere-nah-mah, shri ram (advanced), bam, sha-muth, hi-me, shyama, shiam or shyam, hair-dhign, sharling.[2] I would doubt there are more than a few different lists, hence a very limited number of mantras. Of concern is the fact that several (if not all) are related to Hindu gods. The above are bija (seed) mantras—one word mantras opposed to multi-word mantras. Sir John Wood-roffe, a recognized authority states: "Each mantra has its devata (god); and each devata has its mantra . . . . The most potent way of realizing a devata is with the help of the bija-mantra,'' and ''a mantra may or may not convey on its face its meaning. Bijas have no meaning according to the ordinary use of the language and for this reason they have formed the subject of ridicule to those ignorant of the Mantra-sastra. The initiated, however, know that their meaning is the own form (svarupa) of the particular Devatas (gods) whose Mantra they are . . . . And so the Sastra says that they go to Hell who think that the image is merely a stone (or merely a picture of Guru Dev) and that the Mantra is merely a letter of the alphabet . . . . *The Mantra of a Devata is the Devata.''* (our emphasis)[3] The rhythmical vibrations of its sounds transform the worshiper and by striving he can raise its (the god's) form. Woodroffe equates the following bija mantras with Hindu gods: [4] *hrim* is related to Siva and Prakriti (Vishnu as Purusha) and worships the god Bhuvanesvari; *Krim* is related to Brahma and worships Kali; *Ram* is the mantra of the fire god Agni; *Ing* (ieng) is a variant spelling of ''Aim,[5]'' the mantra of Sarasvati, and worships Vani; *shirim,* derivative of srim is the mantra of the god Laksmi and worships it; *thim* is related to the gods Siva and Bhairava and worships them. *Shyama* is possibly related to Krishna, at least it is half of one of Krishna's names.[6] M.H. Harper notes: ''For the Hindu a *mantra* is not a mere formula or a prayer . . . it is the deity itself . . . . The purpose of *japa,* the frequent repetition of the mantra, is to produce the gradual transformation of the personality of the worshiper into that of the worshiped. The more a worshiper advances in his *japa* the more does he partake of the nature of the deity whom he worships, and the less is he himself.[7] Woodroffe notes that the mantra of a god actually reveals the god to the consciousness of the one invoking it, and the mantra is a symbol of the god itself and its power.[8] This is probably why Maharishi says meditating leads one to contact the gods, thereby gaining their help, and even that one sins if one does *not* contact these gods.[9] Woodroffe: ''So the mind which thinks of the Divinity which it worships (Ista-devata) is at length, through continued devotion, transformed into the likeness of that Devata.[10]'' Mantras are clearly recognized as being directly related to Hindu gods—either invoking them, being their names, or representing them.[11] Charlie Lutes, SRM president stated that the TM mantras were "favored names of God.[12]" Patanjali (2:44; 4:1, 2) says "Repetition of sacred words brings you in direct contact with the God you worship," and that psychic powers are acquired by mantra-repetition. Repeating its name over and over awakens (or transfers) these powers. Dr. Glueck has an interesting comment on TM: "It seems increasingly apparent from EEG findings that the mantra is the significant element in the whole process, apparently able to markedly alter brain function within a matter of seconds.[13]" Maharishi himself says that achieving cosmic consciousness through worship is done by "taking the name or form of the god and experiencing it in its subtler states until the mind transcends the subtlest state . . .," a perfect description of the process of TM.[14] Woodroffe: "When the Mantra of a Divinity is uttered there arises the idea of the Deity whose name it is.[15]

Maharishi says mantras have "a meaning and specific purpose," they are "key words which help one to remember the different steps of the yagyas" and yagyas are "specific actions whereby man makes contact with the higher beings (gods) in creation.[16]" These specific acts are done to worship, please and win the favor of the gods, hence gain their power. This is done through TM.[17] He also says TM "is the most important of the yagyas" and through TM eventually all of life's activities are "given over as an offering to the gods.[18]" Yoga authority Eliade, in describing the mantra as the very *being* of the god remarks: "By repeating the *bija mantra* in conformance with the rules, the practitioner incorporates its ontological essence (nature) to himself, assimilates the god . . . into himself in a concrete immediate fashion.[19]" Woodroffe says the purpose of the mantra is to put one in touch with the god, and that contact comes automatically. Mantric vibrations draw the god's attention to you.

Mantra yoga theory teaches an occult correspondence between the mystical letters and sounds of the mantra and certain areas of the body on one hand and these body areas and divine forces in the cosmos on the other. By repeating a mantra you "awaken" all its corresponding forces in the cosmos. Hence each body area has its god and mantra. Gods are said to reside in the chakras (psychic centers) and their power is assimilated as kundalini arises through each chakra.

There are "obstructions" or knots along the way and it is usage of the bija mantras that breaks through the knots and allows the advance of the psychic kundalini.[20] One reason for yoga exercises is to condition the body areas psychically to their corresponding gods. Yoga practice and theory are inseparable.

FOOTNOTES: APPENDIX ONE

1. John Garrett (Delhi, Oriental Publishers), p. 379.

2. From ex-meditators; *Time,* Nov. 3, 1975; *Atlantic Monthly,* Oct. 1975; *Newsweek,'* Jan. 7, 1974; G. Lewis, *What Everyone Should Know About TM,* p. 52; White, *Everything . . .* p. 19; *Washington Post* articles for Sept. 21-24, 1975; *The Ashman File,* KTTV, Los Angeles, Nov. 6, 1975.

3. *The Garland of Letters,* Madras, India: Ganesh & CO., 6th ed. 1974, pp. viii, 260-61.

4. *Ibid.,* Ch. 26, pp. viii, 277.

5. From a sanskrit authority known to Dr. R.B. Fulton, Union Theological Seminary.

6. Woodroffe, *op. cit.,* Ch. 26, pp. 261-5; Hare Krishna and sanskrit devotee.

7. *Gurus, Swamis and Avataras,* (Westminister, 1972), pp. 97-8.

8. Woodroffe, *op. cit.,* p. 277.

9. *Meditations,* pp. 17-18; *On the Bhagavad Gita,* p. 201, commentary 3:9-13.

10. *The Serpent Power,* (Dover 1974), p. 88.

11. See also D. Shah, *The Meditators*, pp. 16-17, 98; Nikhilananda, *The Upanishads*, (Harper, abridged, 1963), p. 372; Rieker, *op. cit.*, pp. 144, 165-6; Vishnudevananda, *op. cit.*, p. 330-1; Tyberg, *The Language of the Gods*, (1970) pp. 15-16; Swami Prabhavananda, *Yoga and Mysticism*, (1973), pp. 54, 79-80.
12. Berkeley, CA, TM Center, July 19, 1975.

13. Bloomfield, *op. cit.*, p. 102.

14. *On the Bhagavad Gita*, pp. 293, 194.

15. *Serpent Power*, p. 86.

16. *On the Bhagavad Gita*, pp. 487-8; *Meditations*, pp. 38, 17-18.

17. *Ibid. Gita*, pp. 194-6, 292-3, 487-8.

18. *Ibid.*, pp. 198, 201 of 3:9-12.
19. *Patanjali and Yoga* (1975), p. 183.
20. *Ibid.*, p. 183; Wood, *op. cit.*, p. 92; Riviere, *op. cit.*, p. 65; Avalon, *The Serpent Power.*

APPENDIX TWO:
TM AND THE OCCULT

TM stems from a tradition of occultism: Hinduism, Astrology, spiritism and a variety of occult practices that are commonplace in India today. A very large section of the Indian population subscribes to at least a belief in, if not actual practice of, magic, and the Hindu Vedas were supernaturally revealed much in the same way a medium receives messages clairvoyantly from the spirits (or demons, as Gasson and others have pointed out).[1] The techniques of yoga are recognized and applied by all schools of occultism and Maharishi says TM "is the technique of becoming a yogi . . . .[2]" (cf. Yoga Appendix) The basis of all occultism —a desire for supernatural power and knowledge opposed to God's will—is clearly found in Hindu occultism, yoga and TM. Maharishi says that TM brings absolute power and occult knowledge—the basis of the occultists' dreams.[3] Few people realize that the TM initiation ceremony has many parallels to standard occult magic ritual.[4] The very goals and methods of both are similar: the contacting of "higher beings" or powers to fulfill the desire of the occultist through occult power received from the demon or "god." A careful reading of the twenty-page TM teachers manual,

The Holy Tradition, and pp. 38-9 of *Meditations of Maharishi* and his *Bhagavad Gita* commentary, 3:9-13, 4:24-5, shows the similarities. In both cases, there is a ceremonial cleansing or purification of the atmosphere. In magic ritual this is to ban undesirable influences, i.e., evil spirit entities. There is the purifying of the mind and body of the participant. Having purified the inner and outer atmospheres, the Invocation begins. The gods and masters are now invoked, be they Hindu or Egyptian with the resultant establishing of a psychic link between them and the evocator. There is the linking of the individual mind to the realm of the cosmic mind or the Absolute. According to TM's *The Holy Tradition:* "The purpose of this invocation is to attune the active mind by directing it toward the great Masters [deities], to the essential nature of their knowledge of Absolute Being. From that level the mantra is picked up and passed on to the new initiate thereby leading his consciousness to that same field of transcendental Being . . . several times so that more and more of its abundance [power] is incorporated into his life." These psychic links are established as vehicles for transference of occult power, via the ritual, to the teacher or initiate. Both ceremonies involve the complete surrender of the participant—be it to the possessing deity in magic ritual or to the "dead" Guru Dev in TM. Both use incense. I'm not sure of its intended use in TM (although at times the presence of demons is accompanied by a particularly bad odor), but in magic ritual it has a psychological effect and is as capable of allowing demons to assume tangible form as the blood rituals used for the same purpose. Both use continuous repetition of a mantra (the puja is one long mantra). In the magicians' case to induce temporary insanity, the "sweet madness," which culminates in the loss of reason and subsequent possession by the "god-form." Possession does not occur, apparently, in TM initiation. In both cases there are memorized, ritualized physical movements that accompany the ceremony, in TM done only by the teacher. In both there is the surge of psychic force felt by the participant, generally true only for the TM teacher. In both there is the presence of the altar of worship, the offerings placed upon it, the kneeling down before it. Often in magic ritual, there is something on the altar designed to psychically link the person's mind with the ancient tradition—an ancient relic, temple photograph, etc. This is designed to link the mind to the occult knowledge of the tradition being invoked, leading to occult power and knowledge. In TM, the altar picture of Guru Dev, *the yantra*, is combined with the mantra to "successfully finish the job of desensitizing the mind to all alien thought systems and of transplanting the mind from one cultural system to another . . . . 5" The function of using the yantra and mantra is to induce passive, psychically receptive mental states and is so used in a number of cults. The very term "Brahman" means "the productive power in a magical spell. 6"

In magic rituals there may be recognition of the necessity for relaxation of mind and body through singular nostril breathing, an advanced TM technique, as well as a reliance on certain types of sound rhythms (e.g. mantras) to influence the astral world. 7 In TM: "We do something here according to Vedic rites, particular specific chanting to produce an effect in some other world, draw the attention of those higher beings or gods living there. The entire knowledge of the mantras or hymns of the Vedas is devoted to man's connection, to man's communication with the higher beings in different strata of creation.8" Maharishi says that contacting these gods is very beneficial and it is even sinful not to contact them.9 They are more than simply impersonal powers in nature. Maharishi calls them "more evolved beings.10"

TM places the individual in a state of physical immobility and mentally deep passivity, two of the basic requirements for mediumship. The physiological immobilization in some ways may be more profound than sleep. 11 Yogananda notes that cosmic consciousness cannot be maintained initially, "except in the immobile trance state. 12" Maharishi warns against mediumship as a low spiritual path, though its possibility cannot be ruled out for a small percentage of meditators. Ex-medium Raphael Gasson describes how one becomes a medium: "In any case the student is learning to relax his body and to keep his mind on one thing until he has reached a state of what could be regarded as self-hypnosis and passivity, which results in his not thinking for himself. [This is basically TM.] He becomes an automaton through which evil spirits work by taking advantage of his passivity.13" The mental state that mediums have described while in trance possession is similar to advanced TM levels: the oneness of everything, non-existence of time concepts, etc.[14] In fact, the states Maharishi has described are close to those described by mediums such as Mrs. Willett and Eileen Garrett.[15] It is noteworthy also that a very gradual easing back into normal consciousness is absolutely necessary for both mediumship and TM, lest there be a mild to violent shock from too sudden a transference from the profound depths of the mind back to normality.[16] Sri Krishna Prem warns that "dangerous mediumistic psychisms or neurotic dissociations of personality," even insanity, can result from meditation unless certain preparatory qualifications are met, none of which are in TM.[17]

The existence of demons is quite adequately proven from Biblical and occult records. Refusing to believe in them only leaves one open to their manipulation. Dr. Elmer Green of the Menninger Foundation, a physicist and one of the leading neuropsychiatrists in the U.S. says the evidence of thousands of years experience is not to be taken lightly. In noting the very real dangers he warns that psychic exploration can bring one "to the attention of indigenous beings" some of whom are "malicious, cruel, and cunning." They can obsess and even possess people by disrupting the nervous system and controlling the brain. That Dr. Green sees great danger here should be a warning to all.[18] TM does have its cases of spirit contact. In Hinduism, the departed Master often reappears to the favored disciple to guide him. This was true for Yogananda, the founder of the Self Realization Fellowship, for Shankara, and I suspect it is true for Maharishi.[19] Two of Maharishi's books are said to come "as blessings from" Guru Dev. In the Gita commentary, the wisdom therein was "a gift" from Dev and he was its "inspiration and guiding light." It is relevant that Maharishi asserts that contact with the dead is beneficial because one receives their blessing and help.[20] Mr. Lutes' statement about Guru Dev or Maharishi appearing to suicide victims in future lives shows that spirit contact is acceptable within TM beliefs. That Maharishi encourages even young children to contact the dead is highly irresponsible.[21] All this is spiritism and mediumism and to encourage its use by anyone, let alone children, is deplorable. The Bible (Deuteronomy 18:10-13) as well as numerous theologians and psychotherapists have warned of the dangers involved here.[22]

Dr. Koch, who personally has counseled over twenty thousand people involved in the occult, states: "The family histories and the end of these occult workers are, in many cases known to me, so tragic that we can no longer speak in terms of coincidence.[23]"

While actual possession from TM has not been widely publicized, there are known cases. Occultists warn that those who *seek* without knowing what is sought can become prime targets for evil spirits. Meditation of the non-TM variety, still Eastern, has induced possession and near insanity.[24] Meditation, including TM, can induce automatic writing and painting which require possession for their occurrence.[25] It is significant that the very demons[26] which mediums communicate with urge their subjects to practice meditation of the Eastern variety—even saying that it is the very key to spirit contact. This meditation is at times quite parallel to the TM variety, complete with required use of mantras.[27] Is it a coincidence that some of the teachings of the spirits are quite parallel to those of Maharishi?[28] In TM you are advised to sit back and let "whatever happens naturally during the practice simply happen." It is this "opening up" in a passive state which means possession cannot be ruled out. Kent Philpott in his *Manual of Demonology and the Occult* lists at least one case of TM related demon possession and says he has found numerous instances of middle class people becoming demon possessed from yoga exercises, meditation, mind awareness or expansion groups.[29] India-born and educated Doug Shah says being taken over by an evil spirit in TM "is a very real possibility." He notes that in India, "the entire being of the worshiper" may be infused by the god worshiped during puja rituals.[30] Insofar as TM mantras represent or worship Hindu gods, the meditator should be warned (appendix). I personally talked at length with one meditator who, via TM-induced astral projection, came in contact with extremely vicious spirits who would physically beat him up at his slightest disobedience. They literally controlled his life and he could do nothing without their permission. They expressly warned him of the consequences of talking with a Christian. This occurred after only six months of TM. TM teacher Dave Birdsell of Connecticut stated it is not uncommon for advancing meditators to have experiences of objects and people psychically merging with them.[31]

Since Maharishi is himself psychic, it is not surprising that he urges people to develop psychic powers via TM. It is clear that Maharishi is familiar with occult terms and he reportedly has the capacity of mind reading, telepathy, psychic perception of auras and probably many others.32 Maharishi is a man of great occult power which can at times be felt in his presence.33 It is interesting that Idries Shah, noted authority on oriental magic says: "It is true that the Sadhus [Indian holy men] claim that their [psychic] power comes exclusively from spirits; that they within themselves possess no special abilities except that of concentration.34 " Maharishi is no exception, although he might deny it. Also, recent research has indicated, though not much is certain, that transcendental type meditation EEG states have much in common with EEG patterns observed during successful telepathy. Thus TM might produce brain waves of a frequency conducive to telepathy or other occult abilities.35 Psychic powers are induced, either via demonic spirits, as in Indries Shah above, or possibly by the demons opening a latent potential in man, which becomes controlled and manipulated by them for their purposes. Psychic abilities are universally used in opposition to God's will (they are different from miracles done *by* the Holy Spirit *through* Christians) since they never honor Jesus Christ, nor do psychic-occultists ever hold to the Biblical revelation. Most psychics admit that their powers will be taken away from them if they are used outside the conditions stipulated by the spirits, conditions which keep the psychics convinced they are doing good when in fact they are doing great harm because they are using demonic power, not divine power.36 Edgar Cayce is a prime example. Against his better judgement, he developed psychic abilities, which he suspected were satanic, but used them for the "good" they did. He ruined thousands of lives, as well as his own.37 Satan will give just about anyone power, peace, etc., to keep them from the salvation in Jesus Christ. Evil spirits often masquerade as good spirits and do good things for people to deceive them about Biblical truth and salvation. (2 Cor. 11:13-15) Meditation is generally acknowledged as producing the entire range of psychic abilities sooner or later and TM-induced psychic abilities include astral projection, past lives experiences, spirit contact and many others.38 In TM, at the cosmic consciousness level or sooner, occult powers are attained. Maharishi extends an invitation to all men throughout the world "to rise and start the practice of transcendental deep meditation" to develop these powers, claiming that they are *easily* developed via TM.[39] He is being most irresponsible in this, since most all yogis and occultists warn against the dangers involved, though they themselves are often the victims.[40] Psychic powers are sharp traps that rip and tear the psyches of those who pull away. Occultism is littered with accounts of self-glorification, regressive mental states, possession, morbidity, ruined lives, insanity, suicide, etc. If power corrupts, then supernatural power corrupts superlatively, and only the very unwise ignore that warning.

It is very significant that the Ananda Marga Yoga Society publishes a small book, Charya Charya Part II which lists the occult symptoms associated with the rising of the kundalini or serpent power (appendix). These descriptions are very similar to demon possession and severe forms of TM unstressing.

Finally, in Maharishi's writings we find such concepts as the Akashic Records, longtime mainstay of occultism and magic. Believed to be a realm of occult knowledge that one can "tune into," they are in fact a disguise for demonic inspiration.[41] Maharishi seemingly urges a worldwide movement into parapsychology and occultism, not too unusual since their goals and those of TM are the same— supernatural power and knowledge that oppose God's will.[42] Doing things that are opposed to God's will has never been safe and never will be. (Rev. 21:8) The evidence for the truth of Christianity is there—and it should be investigated.[43]

Spiritual seeking in a blind, unreasoned way is extremely dangerous. Eric Utne, publisher and editor of *The New Age Journal* says: "Spiritual seeking has clearly reached the proportions of a national trend. Everyone seems to be looking for the answer. So were the people of Germany during the twenties when there was a widespread fascination with the occult and a higher rate of Indian gurus per capita than even in the U.S. today.[44]" Books such as Angebert's *The Occult and the Third Reich;* Ravenscroft's *The Spear of Destiny;* Brennan's *The Occult Reich,* and others clearly show that Naziism was founded on and supported by occultism and Eastern mysticism of the TM variety. Hitler was in fact fascinated with Eastern mysticism, and was a possessed medium whose ideas of a master race were more based upon personal "higher consciousness" type experiences than Nietzsche's philosophy.[45] The lesson is clear. TM is potentially opening the door of occultism and a psychic elite in society. Let us keep the door shut.

FOOTNOTES: APPENDIX TWO

1. Indries Shah, *Oriental Magic*, Ch. 12, 13; Prem, *The Yoga of the Bhagavad Gita* (1958), p. 204; P. Yogananda, *Autobiography of a Yogi* (1973), pp. 86-7) Gasson, *The Challenging Counterfeit;* V. Ernest, *I Talked with Spirits;* M. Eliade, *Yoga, Immortality and Freedom*, siddhi references, esp. pp. 85-90.

2. *On the Bhagavad Gita*, p. 389; Gaynor, *The Dictionary of Mysticism* (Citadel, 1968), p. 206.

3. *Transcendental Meditation*, pp. 33 (The Basis), 82, 99, 216, 259, 264.

5. Conway, *Magic: An Occult Primer*, pp. 30, 51, 78, 112-47; Prem, *op. cit.*, p. 99; C. Muses, A. Young, *Consciousness and Reality*, pp. 9-17; Naranjo, *op. cit.*, p. 159-60; Shah, *op. cit.*, Ch. 12-13; Doreen Valiente, *An ABC of Witchcraft* (1973); *Rosicrucian Digest*, Feb. 1976, p. 16, notes their use of TM principles.

5. White, ed., *What Is Meditation*, H. Chaudhuri, "Meditation: The Dangers and Rewards," p. 201. This is a reference to White, *Everything . . .*, p. 74.

6. T.W. Organ, *Hinduism, Its Historical Development* (Barron, 1974), p. 82.

7. Conway, *op. cit.*, pp. 61, 74-5.

8. Maharishi, *Meditations*, pp. 17-18.

9. *On the Bhagavad Gita*, pp. 194, 201.

10. *Ibid.*, p. 195.

11. *Journal of Transpersonal Psychology*, 1971, #1, "Meditation as Meta Therapy," pp. 12, 19; *On Bhagavad Gita*, pp. 393; 45, 93; *Transcendental Meditation*, p. 195.

12. *Autobiography*, (1973), p. 477n.

13. R. Gasson, *The Challenging Counterfiet* (Logos, 1970), p. 83.

14. L. Leshan, *How to Meditate* (Bantam, 1975), pp. 126-8; K. Philpott, *A Manual of Demonology and the Occult*, pp. 43, 138.

15. White, ed., *The Highest State of Consciousness*, W.G. Roll, "Psychical Research in Relation to Higher States of Consciousness," pp. 458-62.

16. Twigg, *The Woman Who Stunned the World: Eng Twigg, Medium* (Manor, 1973), p. 38; *Transcendental Meditation*, pp. 53-5.

17. Prem, *op. cit.*, pp. 45-7.

18. *Journal of Transpersonal Psychology*, "On the Meaning of Transpersonal: Some Metaphysical Perspectives," 1971, #1, pp. 39-40.

19. *The Holy Tradition*, p. 16; *Autobiography of a Yogi*.

20. See dedications; *On the Bhagavad Gita*, pp. 5, 16, 21, 194-5, 67, 460-61.

21. *On the Bhagavad Gita*, p. 67 and Note 20.

22. See the appropriate writings of Drs. Kurt Koch, Merril Unger, John W. Montgomery and Walter Martin; Koch, *Christian Counseling and Occultism* (Kregel, 1972), pp. 184-9.

24. M.E.P. Baker, *Meditation: A Step Beyond With Edgar Cayce* (Pinnacle, 1975), pp. 109-111.

25. *Ibid.*, pp. 113-6; personal correspondence with meditators.

26. R. Gasson, *The Challenging Counterfeit;* V. Ernest, *I Talked With Spirits.*

27. Lehmann Hisey, *Key to Inner Space* (Avon, 1975), pp. 20-21; Cooke, *The Jewel in the Lotus* (1973), pp. 17, 19-22, 83, 86-7, 91.

28. Hisey, *op. cit.*, pp. 176, 210, 231; Cook, *op. cit.*, pp. 21-22; Douglas M. Baker, *Superconscious Experience Through Meditation*, nd. no pub.

29. Philpott, *op. cit.*, pp. 33-7, 44.

30. Shah, *op. cit.*, pp. 102, 119.

31. Told to me by Tim J. Runkel of Brown University, March, 1976.

32. *On the Bh. Gita*, p. 29; *Meditations*, pp. 73, 84; White, *Everything . . .*, p. 126; personal correspondence with meditators.

33. Merv Griffin TV special, with Maharishi, Clint Eastwood, etc., late 1975 (Nov.-Dec.)

34. Shah, *Oriental Magic* (1973), p. 123.

35. Lyall Watson, *Supernature* (Bantam, 1974), pp. 230-35,

36. See Gasson's *The Challenging Counterfeit*, Unger's *Demonology in the World Today*.

37. See the biography, *Edgar Cayce, Mystery Man of Miracles*, Swihart, *Edgar Cayce, Reincarnation and the Bible;* Bjornstad, *Twentieth Century Prophecy*, and the *Sorcery in America* series, Vol. 2, by Gordon Lindsey, P.O. Box 24910, Dallas, 75224.

38. White, *Everything . . .*, pp. 126-7; Hammond, *The Search for Psychic Power*, (Bantam, 1975), p. 222; Zaffuto, *Alphagenics* (Warner, 1975), p. 34; LeShan, *op. cit.*, p. 49; White, ed., *What Is Meditation*, pp. 213-7; and many others. Also, *On the Bhagavad Gita*, pp. 194-201.

39. Maharishi, *Transcendental Meditation*, pp. 98-100, 215, 230 with pp. 56, 99, etc.

40. Eliade, *op. cit.*, pp. 88-90.

41. *The Holy Tradition*, p. 13; with *Transcendental Meditation*, p. 33 (the basis).

42. Maharishi, *Transcendental Meditation*, pp. 32-5, 98-100.

43. Josh McDowell, *Evidence That Demands A Verdict;* F. Schaeffer, *He Is There And He Is Not Silent;* Montgomery, *Christianity for the Tough Minded;* Pinnock, *Set Forth Your Case;* Wilbur Smith,

Therefore Stand; H. Morris, *Many Infallible Proofs;* Purtill, *Reason to Believe,* etc.

44. *The New Age Journal,* #8, Oct. 15, 1975, p. 2

45. E.g., Angebert (McGraw-Hill, 1975), p. xi, xiii, 163, 194-200, 278, etc.; Ravenscroft, (Bantam, 1974), p. 25-33, 49, 58, 91, 95-6, 154-68, 172-3, 243-51, 288-93; Brennan; Pauwels and Bergier, *Morning of the Magicians,* part II.

APPENDIX THREE
TM, YOGA, AND THE SERPENT POWER

Other TM proponents, as well as Maharishi, say TM is not yoga; but again, this is not true. The goal of both is Hindu God-realization.[1] Various schools of yoga overlap in their beliefs and practices, hence, TM incorporates parts of karma, raja, mantra and even hatha yoga.[2] Maharishi calls TM karma yoga, and the karma yoga of the Bhagavad Gita involves an unattached, disinterested performance of one's duties. One detaches himself from his acts and their consequences, acts impersonally, without desire and hence absolves his karma. This is TM. One continues to act, but in detachment.[3] Advanced TM courses offer six to twelve month instructions in yoga postures and breathing techniques. Maharishi says, "it is through yoga alone that knowledge steps into practical life," and, "the technique of transcendental meditation, which helps the mind transcend sankalpa [desire], is the technique of becoming a yogi or a sanyasi [recluse, another valid path].[4]" Hence TM is yoga and produces yogis. We should note with the authority Avalon that yoga and magic go hand in hand.[5] Meditation is the operative principle of yoga.

In the authoritative yoga literature there are invariably

warnings about the dangers of yoga practice without *first* gaining vigorous moral, mental and physical prerequisites [*yama* and *niyama*]. This is largely neglected by many today.

Shree Purohit Swami warns: "People forget that Yama and Niyama form the foundation, and unless it is firmly laid, they should not practice postures and breathing exercises., In India and Europe, I came across some three hundred people who suffered permanently from wrong practices, the doctors on examination found that there was nothing organically wrong and consequently could not prescribe.6" H. Rieker warns: "Yoga is not a trifling jest if we consider that any misunderstanding in the practice of yoga can mean death or insanity," and that in kundalini yoga, if the breath is "prematurely exhausted, there is immediate danger of death for the yogi.7" It is symptomatic that in the West we do yoga to *gain* what the East requires as basic prerequisites for even starting yoga; physical and mental health. Yoga is never really removed from its culture (Hinduism) and theory, and those who think they do only postures and breathing are courting dangers. Swami Prabhavananda's *Yoga and Mysticism* gives brain injury, incurable disease and insanity as potential hazards of wrong yoga practice; Rieker lists cancer of the throat, death, "all kinds of ailments," blackouts, strange trance states, death or insanity from "the slightest mistake . . . ." Once we really embark upon yoga, however, the evasion of a single requirement can turn nectar into poison. E. Wood warns of "the imminent risk of most serious bodily disorder, disease and even madness. Many people have brought upon themselves incurable illness and even madness" by neglecting Hatha Yoga prerequisites, and "by any mistake there arises cough, asthma, head, eye and ear pains and many other diseases.8" The Hatha Yoga Pradipika (2:15) says: "Just as lions, elephants and tigers are tamed, so the prana [breath] should be kept under control. Otherwise it can kill the practitioner." Yoga texts have many such warnings. You can see the problems involved when Wood says: "all Hatha Yogas are extremely dangerous," and urges use of raja yoga, while Rieker says "Mastery of Hatha Yoga is only a preliminary to the mastery of raja yoga.9" Insofar as TM and yoga are *defined or thought of* as totally safe, we should not expect to hear much of harmful cases since their cause is thought to be elsewhere.

Yoga is really pure occultism as any number of yoga and occult texts prove.[10] Occult abilities are very common from yoga practice and the numerous dangers of occultism are evident from many studies.[11] The yoga scholar and sanskrit authority Mishra states: "In conclusion, it may be said that behind every psychic investigation, behind mysticism, occultism, etc., knowingly or unknowingly, the yoga system is present.[12]"

Kundalini is thought of as a female serpent lying dormant at the base of the spine. When aroused via yoga she travels up the spine, opening the *chakras* (psychic centers) and leads to union with Brahman. "Traditionally she is known as Durga the creatrix, Chandi the fierce and blood-thirsty, and Kali the destroyer. She is also Bhajangi the serpent. As Chandli or Kali she has a garland of skulls around her neck and drinks human blood.[13]" You don't fool carelessly with kundalini—unless you care for terrible body pain and heat, deteriorating health, numerous forms of insanity or sudden death.[14] Shree Purohit Swami experienced near insanity, ate the leaves of two entire nimba trees, devoured insipid mudra leaves and could not sit or stand. He mentions one yogi who had the fire rage for six to eight months, another who had to sit under cold tap water eight hours a day.[15] Gopi Krishna, founder of one of the several Kundalini research centers in the world records his kundalini experience: "It was variable for many years, painful, obsessive, even phantasmic. I have passed through almost all the stages of different mediumistic, psychotic and other types of mind, for sometime I was hovering between sanity and insanity. I was writing in many languages, some of which I never knew" [the mediumistic ability of automatic writing].[16] He believes most schizophrenics and manic-depressives probably represent malfunctioning kundalini, notes the ease with which it produces mental derangement, and mentions his personal encounters with cases of kundalini-caused insanity. He notes that in India it is widely known that Hatha Yoga practices can lead to insanity.[17] "The power, when aroused in a body not attuned to it with the help of various disciplines or not genetically mature for it, can lead to awful mental states, to almost every form of mental disorder, from hardly noticeable aberrations to the most horrible forms of insanity, to neuroses and paranoia, to megalomania, and, by causing tormenting pressure on reproductive organs, to an all-consuming sexual thirst that is never assuaged.[18]" It is noteworthy that kundalini, mediumistic and possession states have common characteristics including various occult manifestations and the demonic succubae.[19]

We believe that TM has the potential for arousing kundalini. It is generally thought to be aroused only by specific procedures with specific accompanying signs. Yet many occult groups use different methods to arouse kundalini (e.g. Edgar Cayce's method is not Avalon's[20]), *while the results are similar,* showing arousal occurs in various ways. Hence "kundalini" is simply another guise for demonic activity, allowing demons to achieve their purposes by various methods. TM may not involve "classic" kundalini arousal, but there are numerous similarities. Kundalini generally takes several years to reach the top chakra, TM takes five years for cosmic consciousness. TM may be a slower arousal, though spontaneous or accidental arousal is not to be ruled out. Rieker: "Kundalini is the mainstay of all yoga practices.[21]" Avalon says *all* mantras are manifestations of Kundalini, being the basis of arousing her.[22] (He also notes that mantras *are* psychic powers which lend themselves to impartial use, "A man may be injured or killed by Mantra.[23]" This is the occult power of black magic where the occultist can injure or kill others. Dr. Koch, in *Between Christ and Satan,* lists several examples. Even Maharishi describes what sounds like TM-induced kundalini.[24] Both TM and kundalini have produced the following (based on interviews with meditators, ex-TM teachers, TM researchers and the footnotes): sexual arousal to the point of free prostitution, blackouts, surges of power, past lives experiences, demonic and insane states, temporary respiration stoppage, astral projection, the development of "soma," occult powers, including an opening to the astral world, akashic records, spirit contact, and extreme paranoia. There is a similarity in claims and in description of mental states attained through the practice (bliss, merging or unity, enhanced perception, ego dissolution, mystical contemplation, union in Brahman, etc.), similar practices used (mantra meditation, sensory withdrawal, nostril breathing), and, finally, identity change.[25] On the point of sexual arousal, a severe warning is necessary. Sri Krishna Prem says, "It is safer to play with dynamite than to practice the *yoga* of meditation" without complete control of inner and outer sex drives. A. Avalon warns that intercourse during the early stages of Hatha Yoga "is likely to prove fatal.26" Finally, Dave Haddon, who comes out of an extensive background in tantric yoga theory and practice states:

"At first glance it is difficult to pinpoint such a thing as 'kundalini arousal' in TM. However, if we look in depth at one central feature of the practice, the initiation, as well as some of the less publicized techniques which are taught by the movement, we may be led to conclude that TM, as a yoga technique, is indeed involved with stimulating the psychic *kundalini*, whether practitioners believe in the existence of it or not.

"*Vedic* initiation ceremonies, of the type employed by TM, are traditionally regarded as functioning at two levels. Superficially, as the translation of TM's hymn of worship (*puja*) reveals, the initiator involves himself in obeisance to various deities (*devatas*), veneration of the tradition by which the mantras are delivered to him, and invocation and worship of that tradition as embodied in Guru Dev, who is recognized both as a self-realized expressions of divinity, as well as the bestower of the *siddhi* (power) of the lineage he represents. At this level, the TM initiation ceremony exists to bring the *siddhi* of the line of Shankara to bear upon the deliverance of the *mantra*. As M.P. Pandit writes in his translation and commentary on *The Preliminary Sutras of Parashurama,* 'The *Mantra* must be backed up by a tradition, *guruparampara.* That is, it must have behind it the spiritual energism imparted by a whole line of practicants, from successive *Guru* to *sisya,* teacher to disciple. So handed down it is charged with a special dynamism and contains the essence of the *tapasya,* askesis (purification) of all the *upasakas,* (practitioners) that have gone before.'What is apparently a ritual ceremony of worship, then, is but the outward face of what is really a transmission of psycho/spiritual power. This is the 'inner meaning' of the TM ceremony, which transforms 'initiation' (as understood in the West) into spiritual *diksa,* which, again according to Pandit, is a 'process that launches one on the path of Realization

210

and hence is of capital importance in spiritual life. By *diksa,* initiation, the Teacher implants in the disciple the seed of Realization, communicates the necessary power to effect the fruition.'

"Such *diksa* is commonly understood to have the result of awakening the dormant psychic potentiality of an individual—the *kulakundalini-shakti.* Whether this awakening [*shakti-pat*] is the actual focus of the TM initiation is unclear, although it is likely. The definitions of 'cosmic consciousness,' 'God consciousness,' and 'unity consciousness' which Maharishi offers to describe the states attainable through TM correspond quite precisely to traditional Hindu statements about those levels of awareness which are accessible only through the activity of kundalini. In addition, the techniques of *asana* (yoga postures), and *pranayama* (yogic breathing exercises) which are recommended for more advanced TMers, can be most accurately understood in terms of their conditioning the physical and psychic anatomies to be able to receive such energies as released by the aroused *kundalini.* Moreover, the subjective reports of those who have experienced what the TM movement calls 'unstressing,' or 'normalization of the nervous system' (dubious psychological rationalizations at best), are in very many instances identical with the well formulated, traditional descriptions of the 'occult' symptoms' which a meditator can expect to experience as the *kundalini* rises through the various psychic centers [*chakras*].

"If TM *diksa* is indeed what it appears to be, then Maharish Mahesh Yogi, be he *maha-siddha* or charlatan, is acting with the greatest irresponsibility in his wholesale promotion of the technique. The *Vedas, tantra shastras,* as well as most contemporary *gurus*, are in complete accord in strongly warning against indiscriminate *kundalini* arousal. Neurosis, psychosis, and even physical dysfunction leading to death is the projected lot of one who fails to exercise the greatest caution, or to follow the most rigorous discipline, in tapping into the power of *shakti.* The expanding list of 'TM casualties' who suffer from prolonged disorientation, lapses of conscious awareness, and other more severe psychological problems which, in several instances, have resulted in the hospitalization of the meditator, would certainly seem to indicate that there is a force at work in TM which is not wholly within the control of the practitioner, nor which is necessarily amicable to his well-being.[27] ''

FOOTNOTES: APPENDIX THREE

1. Rieker, *The Yoga of Light* (1974), p. 135; Maharishi, *Transcendental Meditation*, p. 249; Vishnudevananda, *The Complete Illustrated Book of Yoga*, pp. ix, 7-9; Robbins, Fisher, *op. cit.*, pp. 138-9.

2. *Creative Intelligence* (TM pub.) #1, pp. 12-13, cf. *On the Bhagavad Gita*, pp. 298, 390; *Transcendental Meditation*, p. 196; A. Avalon, *The Serpent Power*, pp. 185-6.

3. M. Eliade, *Yoga, Immortality and Freedom* (1973), pp. 153-61; *On the Bhagavad Gita*, pp. 319-20.

4. *On the Bhagavad Gita*, pp. 16, 116, 185, 320, 389, 407.

5. Avalon, *op. cit.*, pp. 186, 204.

6. *Aphorisms of Yoga*, (Faber, 1973); pp. 56-7 cf. Feuernstein and Miller, *Yoga and Beyond*, (Schocken, 1972), pp. 7-8, 27-8.

7. *The Yoga of Light*, (Dawn House, 1974), pp. 9, 134.

8. Vedanta Press (1972), pp. 18-19; Rieker, *op. cit.*, pp. 30, 79, 96, 111-12; *Seven Schools of Yoga* (Quest, 1973), pp. 14, 78-9.

9. Wood, *op. cit.*, p. 79; Rieker, *op. cit.*, p. 128.

10. R.S. Mishra, *Yoga Sutras* (Anchor, 1973), pp. 132, 136-7, 295-399; Wood, *op. cit.*, pp. 112-13; Mishra, *Fundamentals of Yoga*, pp. 2-3, Ch. 17-19, 26-7; Ji Brennan, *Astral Doorways*, (Weiser, 1975), pp. 98, 29; H. Chaudhuri, *Philosophy of Meditation*, pp. 50-51.

212

11. K. Koch, *Christian Counseling and Occultism* (1972); Montgomery, *Demon Possession* (1975), etc.

12. *Yoga Sutras*, p. 138.

13. Gopi Krishna, *The Awakening of Kundalini* (Dutton, 1975), p. 13.

14. Rieker, p. 134; Vishnudevananda, p. 328; L. Hisey, *Keys to Inner Space* (Avon, 1975), p. 146; White, *Everything* . . ., p. 99.

15. *Aphorisms of Yoga*, pp. 57-8.

16. Krishna, *op. cit.*, p. 124.

17. *Ibid.*, pp. 14, 33, 37.

18. *Ibid.*, p. 14.

19. *Ibid.*, pp. 19, 37, 47, 82, 94, 120, 123; Rieker, *op. cit.*, pp. 49, 78, 102; J.M. Riviere, *Tantric Yoga* (1973), pp. 64, 68; A. Avalon, *op. cit.*, (1974), pp. 83-84, 242.

20. ARE circulating file on Kundalini; Baker, *Meditation, A Step Beyond with Edgar Cayce*, p. 69; *ARE Journal*, Nov. 1975, pp. 259-63; Puryear, Thurston, *Meditation and the Mind of Man* (1975), p. 80.

21. Rieker, *op. cit.*, p. 101.

22. Avalon, *op. cit.*, pp. 83, 225.

23. *Ibid.*, pp. 83-4, cf. note.

24. *On the Bhagavad Gita*, p. 410.

25. Riviere, *op. cit.*, pp. 64, 68; Krishna, *op. cit.*, pp. 14, 47, 94-100; Hammond, *We Are All Healers* (Ballantine, 1974), pp. 268-9; TM puja, "The Holy Tradition;" *ARE Journal*, Nov. 1975, p. 263; White, *Everything* . . ., pp. 97-9, 127; Vishnudevananda, p. 294; *Transcendental Meditation*, p. 33; M. Eliade, *Patanjali and Yoga*, p. 193; H. Chaudhuri, *op. cit.*, pp. 68, 74-7; Avalon, *The Serpent Power*, pp. 7-10, 18, 19, 127, 144; Rieker, *op. cit.*, p. 133; Prabhavananda, *op. cit.*, pp. 32, 35, 41, 68, Ch. 3; Norvell, *The Miracle Power of Transcendental Meditation*, p. 117, etc.; Rieker, *op. cit.*, pp. 79, 92, 144, 146, 91, 97, 148; Krishna, *op. cit.*, pp. viii, 16, 26, 43-5, 14, 47, 66-7, 72-4, 82, 87-93; Avalon, *op. cit.*, pp. iii, 9, 81-2, 204-8, 214, 222-8, 246-8, 279-80, 291-3, 254-5, 282-3.

26. Avalon, *op. cit.*, p. 190; Prem, *The Yoga of the Bhagavad Gita* (1973), p. 53.

27. Personal correspondence.

213

APPENDIX FOUR:
TM, REINCARNATION, AND THE BIBLE

Maharishi teaches reincarnation, hence it is not surprising that meditators have reported reincarnation experiences. Some people believe the Bible teaches reincarnation; however, the two are really based on entirely opposite principles. Reincarnation states that we pay for our own sins via self-improvement throughout many lives, based on karmic law. If we do evil in this life, we pay for it in the next, but eventually everyone reaches the goal of salvation or liberation. The Bible, on the other hand, says we have one life in which to get things straight with God (Hebrews 9:27), not thousands or millions. We can never be good enough or improve ourselves enough to meet God's holy standard, which is complete perfection. Being God, he can require no less. This is why he sent Jesus Christ—because we *couldn't* meet his perfect standards. Christ died in our place and took the penalty for our sins. The Bible says that self-improvement, or salvation based on human effort alone (e.g. reincarnation), is a hopeless path, and will never take us to God (Galatians 1: 8. 3: 24). The statements of Jesus himself and the writers of the New Testament are clear. Christ came to die for the world's sins, so that through faith (not works) men could come to God. That way, no one can claim they are any better than someone else. (Ephesians 2: 8-9; Luke 24: 25,46; I Peter 2: 24; 4: 1; Hebrews 2: 9, 10, 18; 9: 26). The crucifixion of Jesus was planned from eternity past (Acts 2: 23) and foretold 700 years prior to the event (Isaiah 53). If we can make it on our own, then God made a mistake in judging Jesus in our place, hardly a plausible option. If God is God, he makes no mistakes. He says the penalty of sin is death—physical death as well as spiritual separation from Him. Men die because they sin. Did you ever stop to think *why* man isn't immortal? Perfect men would not die. The very fact that Christ rose from the dead—and this is an historical fact, by all standards of historical judgement and legal evidence[1]—proves all sins were paid for, or else he would still be dead. (Romans 4:25) Christ died because he took the penalty for our sin—death. And he resurrected because the entire penalty for our sin was paid. Hence eternal life, a perfect and *personal* existence forever with an infinitely perfect God, is potentially available to anyone who will believe in Christ. "For God so loved the world that He gave His only Son, that whoever believes in Him might not perish but have everlasting life." (John 3: 16) This is not just religious sentimentality. The evidence for its truthfulness is nearly overwhelming.[2]

So, reincarnation is at its roots opposed to the Biblical message. Yet people do have what they feel are genuine reincarnation experiences. It is most interesting that the occult volume *Oahspe* says these are experiences implanted into the mind by evil spirits for their play. It's no game however. Reincarnation and occultism have long been close friends and most occult schools teach reincarnation. These experiences fall into the realm of spititual warfare—an attempt to lull people into a false belief that there is no coming judgement (Acts 17: 31), but merely a progression into the next life. Demons know that if people really believed that God would hold them responsible for their behavior, and that there would be an accounting before Him, they would be likely to accept God's way and receive Christ rather than to be judged eternally. Hence they devise numerous ways to keep people from believing in the coming judgement, and reincarnation is among them. These experiences are implanted into the mind via demonic power and are very real to the individual who undergoes them. The fallen angels have been around a long time and it is rather easy for them to select some experience out of the past and implant it into a person's consciousness. Some feel these experiences are proof of reincarnation, but the theory has numerous problems, most of them admitted by reincarnationists. It has shown no evidence of working throughout all of man's history, i.e., things should be improving, but the world is, if anything, worse off than ever. Actual proof is impossible by its very nature, (subjective, generally indefinite experiences that are difficult to confirm). There are numerous internal contradictions and a variety of opposing theories, some of which disprove others, e.g., transmigration or progression? There is no way to tell which theory, if any, is correct. It has an uncertain origin historically and its association with negative things like the occult increases the possibility that these are purposefully deceptive experiences. People who have experiences often end up producing information in a trance state, from one of their past lives, and its content is always unbiblical, which is rather a problem when all the evidence points to the truth and validity of the Bible. Historically, India, the country that has believed in reincarnation the most, has suffered the most. The vast majority of people never even remember a single past life. To the extent that suffering, the payment for past evil, causes people to *do* evil, the theory is a failure and self-defeating. Other problems include: 1) In karmic law it is a sin to *stop* suffering, hence a fatalistic acceptance of suffering and evil is the result. 2) Cases of possession during the reincarnation trance experience may occur. 3) How can the inviolate law of karma be held ''in suspension'' for several lifetimes? 4) If ignorance of reincarnation is a hindrance to spiritual progress, as taught by Edgar Cayce and others, why would the soul, prior to inhabiting a body, cause itself to forget about reincanation, thus hindering the very progress it is trying to make? 5) the evidence for it almost always stems from altered or abnormal states of consciousness (hypnosis, drugs, occultism) which are clearly capable of demonic intrusion and manipulation. 6) Its Western form is simply an extension of the scientifically invalid [3] postulate of evolution. Occultist Dr. Cerminara: ''The theory of reincarnation is really the familiar scientific theory of evolution on a psychological and cosmic level.[4]'' 7) The ''spirits'' at seances are more than willing to give information on rein-

216

carnation, and the reasoning goes, they should know, since they are between incarnations. However, their information is contradictory. Finally, for as long as the human race has existed, history records no perfect man, except Jesus Christ, and he repudiated the idea of reincarnation. Hence, the only perfect man ever to live has denied its validity. (John 9:1-3; Matt. 25: 46: Rev. 20: 10-15) Even reincarnationists claim he was more advanced than anyone else—so if anyone should know whether the theory is true, he should. Also, the Biblical records, for which there *is* a great amount of evidence, universally oppose reincarnation: e.g., Phil. 1: 21, 23; II Cor. 5: 1, 4, 8; Heb. 9: 27; 10: 12; Acts 17: 31; Acts 7: 59; Luke 23: 44 (How could a thief not reincarnate?); Psalm 78: 39; II Sam. 12: 23; John 3: 3,4 (obviously not physical); II Cor. 6: 2; Gal. 1: 8-9; 2: 16, 21;3: 2, 3, 10-13, 21, 24, etc.

References: D. Kelsey, J. Grant, *Many Lifetimes;* (Pocket. 1968)

G. Cerminara, *The World Within; [Signet,* 1974)

N. Langley, Edgar Cayce on Reincarnation;

M. Moore, M. Douglas, *Reincarnation Key to Immortality*; (Arcane 1968)

J. Stearn, *Door to the Future*;

L. D. Weatherhead, *The Case for Reincarnation*;

R. Montgomery, *Here and Hereafter*; (Fawcett Crest, 1968)

Reincarnation: An East-West Anthology

Jess Stearn, *Search for A Soul: Taylor Caldwell's Psychic Lives*

B. Steiger, *The Enigma of Reincarnation* (Ace, 1973)

FOOTNOTES: APPENDIX FOUR

1. Josh McDowell, *Evidence That Demands A Verdict;* Frank Morrison, *Who Moved the Stone?;* M. Green, *Man Alive;* James Orr, *The Resurrection.*

2. J. McDowell, *Evidence That Demands A Verdict;* H. Morris, *Many Infallible Proofs;* F. Schaeffer, *He Is There and He Is Not Silent;* W. Smith, *Therefore Stand;* Purtill, *Reasons to Believe.*

3. E.g., R.L. Wysong, *The Creation-Evolution Controversy* (Inquiry Press, East Lansing, Mich., 1976); J.F. Coppedge, *Evolution, Possible or Impossible* (Zondervan, 1975).

4. Cerminara, *op. cit.*, p. 4.